Vegetarian Times LOW-FAT & Fast
Pasta

Also by the editors of Vegetarian Times *magazine*

Vegetarian Times Beginner's Guide (1996)

Vegetarian Times Vegetarian Entertaining (1996)

Vegetarian Times Low-Fat & Fast (1997)

Vegetarian Times
Low-Fat & *Fast*
Pasta

From the Editors of
Vegetarian Times magazine

Macmillan • USA

MACMILLAN

A Simon & Schuster Macmillan Company
1633 Broadway
New York, NY 10019-6785

Library of Congress Cataloging-in-Publication Data

Vegetarian times low-fat & fast pasta / the editors of Vegetarian times
p. cm.

Includes index.

ISBN: 0-02-861728-2 (alk. paper)

1. Cookery (Pasta) 2. Vegetarian cookery. 3 Low-fat diet—
Recipes. 4. Quick and easy cookery. I. Vegetarian times.

TX809.M17V44 1997   97-391
641.8′22—dc21   CIP

Manufactured in the United States of America

10 9 8 7 6 5 4 3 2 1

Contents

Acknowledgments

The editors of Vegetarian Times wish to thank recipe developers *extraordinaire* Karen A. Levin and Jay Solomon for the wonderful recipes in this volume. Thanks to their creativity and imagination, this cookbook offers the reader an essential guide to the pasta possibilities in cuisines from Italian to Southeast Asian.

Thank you to our Macmillan editor Justin Schwartz for his patience and understanding while we put this book together during one of the busiest times in *Vegetarian Times* history, and to *Vegetarian Times* senior editor Karin Horgan Sullivan, who cheerfully and professionally picked up the slack.

Finally, thanks to Terry Christofferson, whose industriousness and dedication never cease to amaze, and to *Vegetarian Times* Group Publisher Toni Apgar, who continues to trust.

—Carol Wiley Lorente,
Special Projects Editor
Vegetarian Times

Introduction

Welcome to Volume 2 of the *Vegetarian Times Low-Fat & Fast* cookbook series: *Low-Fat & Fast Pasta.*

Low-fat cooking has never been more popular. More than ever, people recognize that eating a diet containing less fat and more complex carbohydrates goes a long way toward the prevention of heart disease, diabetes, obesity, high cholesterol, high blood pressure, and the other illnesses that ravage Americans.

We know that you want healthful meals, but you want convenience too. And we know that if you're like more and more Americans, you want those meals to be meatless. How do we know?

Vegetarian Times magazine has been the authority on vegetarianism since its beginnings in 1974. Since instituting the "Low-Fat and Fast" column in *Vegetarian Times* magazine in 1989, it continues to be the most well-read section of our magazine. It's only natural then that we follow it with a cookbook series based on the same premise—tasty, low-fat, vegetarian meals in about thirty minutes or less.

Vegetarian Times Low-Fat & Fast cookbook series is designed for the way health-minded Americans like you want to eat. Each volume contains 150 to 200 delicious recipes that are guaranteed to satisfy your need for healthful eating and your desire to get food on the table fast.

Eating a low-fat diet—and cooking low-fat meals—isn't as difficult as you might think. Our advice has always been to base your meals and snacks on whole grains, beans, fruits, and vegetables; they're naturally low in fat and calories, and they contain all of the vitamins, minerals, and fiber you need.

Pasta, particularly the whole grain varieties, fits the bill on all counts. Wholesome, low in fat, high in complex carbohydrates, and simple to cook, pasta has become the centerpiece of the American plate, particularly for vegetarians, who take advantage of pasta's versatility in combinations too numerable and varied to list.

Not only is pasta available in the customary semolina variety, but supermarkets also are selling pastas made with buckwheat, rice, even bean flours, in fresh or dried versions, and in flavors such as tomato, beet, carrot, or spinach. Pasta is now such a staple of the American diet that experimentation is *de rigueur*. Plain spaghetti becomes a quite different and more sophisticated dish when you select, say, a parsley-garlic variety; a vegetable soup takes on a more creative look when you substitute ditalini for macaroni. Plus, we've included recipes that run the gamut of flavors, from Italian to Southwest, from Japanese to Indian.

Although our recipes suggest what we think is the best pasta to use in each, feel free to substitute. (See the Pasta Glossary, page xi, for definitions of every pasta used in the recipes in this cookbook.) A black pepper fettuccine, for example, can provide an elegant substitute in an Alfredo recipe. And if you're out of macaroni for that macaroni and cheese casserole, well, nothing wrong with using rotini or small shells instead.

For the best results, refer to the package for cooking instructions (and, of course, your own taste). We have provided cooking times in every recipe, but these are general and will differ from brand to brand and from dry to fresh pasta.

FAST FOOD

All of the recipes in this cookbook take around thirty minutes or less to prepare. But getting your own favorite meals on the table also can be easier when you know a few tricks. Most of it boils down to planning and completing tasks as the food cooks. Here are some tips for quick cooking:

- Set out all ingredients and utensils you'll need before you begin cooking, and mentally organize the preparation so you can "dovetail" steps. For example, while the pasta is cooking, chop the garlic and tomatoes for the sauce. (We've written the recipes in this cookbook in such a manner to help you do this.)

- Organize and equip your kitchen to your advantage. Keep frequently used utensils, such as wooden spoons, rubber scrapers, spatulas, and whisks, in a container or drawer next to the stove; keep pots, pans, mixing bowls, and measuring cups nearby. And return these items to the same places so you won't have to hunt for them next time.

— Wholesome, nutritious foods do come in convenient, prepared forms—use them! Frozen vegetables, canned beans, bagged, cut-up, and shredded produce, fresh pastas, canned vegetable broths, and other prepared foods are wholesome and of good quality and save time. Don't forget the supermarket salad bar as a source for cut-up vegetables, and the canned food aisle for prepared garlic, ginger, roasted red peppers, etc.

— There are simple ways to speed the actual heating and cooking of foods. Smaller and thinner cuts of vegetables cook more quickly than thick ones. Wide-diameter skillets and pots speed up heating and simmering. Also, when you need to boil water, start with hot tap water to speed things along. (Every little bit helps!)

ABOUT OUR RECIPES

After each recipe, we provide nutritional information that lists the amount of calories, protein, fat, carbohydrates, cholesterol, sodium, and fiber per serving. When a choice of ingredients is given (as in "skim milk or soy milk"), the analysis reflects the first ingredient listed (skim milk). When there is a range of servings (as in "1 to 2 tablespoons olive oil"), the analysis reflects the first number listed (1 tablespoon). When an ingredient is listed as optional, it is not included in the nutritional analysis.

We do not list the percentage of calories from fat per serving because we believe it is misleading. The percent of fat in a given recipe is less important than the percent of fat eaten in an entire day. The bulk of research indicates that fat intake must be less than 25 percent of calories to prevent disease and to promote health. So if you eat 2,000 calories per day, you can eat 55 grams of fat per day and maintain a diet that obtains 25 percent of calories from fat.

Where appropriate, we also give variations and helpful hints after recipes. Variations suggest other ways of preparing the recipe; helpful hints discuss advance preparation, list how-to's, define terms and ingredients, and tell you where to buy products.

We think you'll find *Vegetarian Times Low-Fat & Fast Pasta* an invaluable guide to cooking fast, healthful, vegetarian meals. Happy cooking.

Pasta Glossary

Here is a guide to the 55 pasta shapes
included in the recipes in this book:

Acini di Peppe   Tiny pasta shaped like peppercorns. Also called tubettini.

Alphabets   Small pasta in the shape of letters.

Angel-Hair   *See Capellini.*

Bow Tie Pasta   A medium-size pasta shaped like bow ties. Also called farfalle.

Buckwheat Noodles   *See Soba.*

Capellini   Thin spaghetti. Also called angel-hair.

Cavatappi   Short, ridged corkscrew macaroni.

Cavatelli   Short, narrow shell pasta with rippled edges.

Cellophane Noodles   Clear Asian noodles made from mung bean starch. They do not need to be cooked; just a soak in hot water will do. Also called Chinese vermicelli.

Chinese or Japanese Curly Noodles   *See Chuka Soba.*

Chinese Vermicelli   *See Cellophane Noodles.*

Chuka Soba   Wheat noodles. Also called ramen or Chinese or Japanese curly noodles.

Conchiglie   Italian for "seashells"; name for seashell-shaped pasta. Also called soup shells.

Conchigliette Piccole Miniature conchiglie.

Ditalini   Very short macaroni.

Farfalle   *See Bow Tie Pasta.*

Fettuccine   Long, flat noodles about $3/8$ inch wide.

Fusilli   Spiral spaghetti from $1\frac{1}{2}$ to 12 inches long; also spelled fusille.

Galetti   Small pasta shapes that look like a scroll rolled inward on both ends.

Gemelli   Italian for "twins," these are short twists that look like two strands of spaghetti twisted together.

Gnocchi   Small dumpling-type pasta made of potato dough.

Linguine   Flat spaghetti, not as wide as fettuccine.

Lo Mein   Long Chinese noodles made from wheat flour, similar in size to fettuccine.

Macaroni   Little elbows.

Manicotti   Large tubes of pasta that are cooked and then stuffed.

Mostaccioli   Italian for "mustaches," these are tubes of pasta about two inches long that are cut on the diagonal.

Mostacciolini   Small mostaccioli.

Orecchiette   Italian for "little ears," these resemble little derby hats or disks.

Orzo   Rice-shaped pasta.

Pagodas   Small radiatore pasta.

Pappardelle   Wide noodles with ruffled sides.

Penne   Large tubes cut on the diagonal. They are available plain or ridged (called penne rigate).

Penne Rigate   Ridged penne.

Perciatelli   Hollow spaghetti.

Radiatore   Small pasta shaped like little radiators.

Ramen   *See Chuka Soba.*

Ravioli   Small pasta squares stuffed with various fillings.

Rice Noodles   Very long, thin, translucent noodles. Two types are rice sticks and rice vermicelli.

Rice Sticks   Rice-flour noodles shaped like fettuccine or linguine; sold in cellophane packages.

Rice Vermicelli   Thin, hairlike spaghetti made from rice flour.

Rigatoni   Short, ridged, tube-shaped pasta.

Rotelle   Round pasta with spokes that resemble wagon wheels. Also called wagon wheel pasta.

Rotini   Short spirals of spaghetti.

Soba   Flat, grayish-brown Japanese noodles made from wheat and/or buckwheat. Also called buckwheat noodles.

Somen   Thin wheat noodles similar to vermicelli.

Soup Shells   *See Conchiglie.*

Spaghetti   Long, round strands of pasta.

Tagliatelle   Narrow fettuccine, about $1/4$ inch wide.

Tortellini   Ring-shaped pasta stuffed with various fillings.

Tubetti   Tiny tube shapes.

Tubettini   *See Acini di Peppe.*

Udon   Japanese wheat noodles, almost the thickness of spaghetti.

Vermicelli   Very thin, hairlike spaghetti.

Wagon Wheels   *See Rotelle.*

Ziti   Long, thin tubes of pasta.

CHAPTER 1

Main Dishes

Southwestern Minestrone with Corn Macaroni

This intriguing variation of the Italian soup classic is a tureen of black beans, corn, vegetables, and assertive Southwestern spices. This is an ideal opportunity to try a specialty macaroni made with either corn, spelt, or quinoa.

1 tablespoon canola oil
1 medium yellow onion, diced
1 red or green bell pepper,
    seeded and diced
4 cloves garlic, minced
1 jalapeño pepper, seeded and
    minced
6 cups vegetable broth
¼ cup canned tomato paste
2 teaspoons dried oregano
1½ teaspoons ground cumin
½ teaspoon freshly ground
    black pepper
½ teaspoon salt
1 cup corn macaroni (or spelt or
    quinoa macaroni)
1½ cups corn kernels, fresh or
    frozen
1 cup cooked (or canned) and
    drained black beans
¼ cup chopped fresh parsley

In a large saucepan, heat the oil over medium-high heat. Add the onion, bell pepper, garlic, and jalapeño pepper and cook, stirring, for 7 minutes.

Add the vegetable broth, tomato paste, oregano, cumin, pepper, and salt, and bring to a simmer, stirring occasionally. Stir in the macaroni, corn, beans, and parsley, and return to a simmer. Cook, stirring occasionally, until the pasta is al dente, about 5 to 7 minutes. Remove from the heat and let stand for 5 to 10 minutes before serving.

Ladle the soup into shallow bowls and serve with warmed flour tortillas.

Makes 6 servings

VARIATIONS

Add 2 tablespoons of chopped cilantro in place of the parsley or offer shredded Monterey Jack cheese as a garnish (about 1 tablespoon per serving).

Per Serving:
230 Calories; 9g Protein; 4g Fat;
44g Carbohydrates; 0 Cholesterol;
1,356mg Sodium; 8g Fiber.

Conchiglie with Salsa Cruda di Pomodoro

This dish features luscious vine-ripened tomatoes (called pomodoro in Italian). Since it is an uncooked sauce, choose the best and brightest tomatoes available.

4 or 5 large tomatoes, coarsely chopped
1 cup cooked chickpeas
¼ cup chopped basil (sliced chiffonade-style; see Helpful Hint)
¼ cup chopped fresh parsley
2 cloves garlic, minced
1 tablespoon olive oil
1 tablespoon balsamic vinegar
½ teaspoon freshly ground black pepper
½ teaspoon salt
8 ounces conchiglie (medium shells) or orecchiette
¼ cup freshly grated Parmesan cheese (optional)

Place the chopped tomatoes in a colander and let drain for about 1 minute, stirring at least once. Transfer the tomatoes to a large serving bowl and combine with all of the remaining ingredients except the pasta and cheese. Let stand at room temperature until the pasta is ready.

In a large saucepan, bring 3 quarts of water to a boil over medium-high heat. Place the shells in the boiling water, stir, and return to a boil. Cook until al dente, 9 to 11 minutes, stirring occasionally. Drain the pasta in a colander and shake well to remove the excess water.

Fold the shells into the tomato sauce and serve at once. If desired, offer the Parmesan cheese as a condiment at the table.

Makes 4 servings

Helpful Hint

To cut chiffonade-style, stack and roll the basil leaves into a cigarlike shape. Slice the leaves widthwise, creating thin "ribbons."

Per Serving:
276 Calories; 10g Protein; 5g Fat; 48g Carbohydrates; 0 Cholesterol; 308mg Sodium; 2g Fiber.

Cheese Ravioli with Triple Pepper Red Sauce

The piquant nature of this robust red sauce is tastefully juxtaposed against the creamy flavors and textures of cheese ravioli.

1 tablespoon canola oil
1 medium yellow onion, slivered
1 large green bell pepper, seeded and cut into narrow strips
2 or 3 cloves garlic, minced
1 Hungarian wax pepper, seeded and minced
1 jalapeño pepper, seeded and minced
One 28-ounce can tomato puree
One 14-ounce can stewed tomatoes
½ cup water
2 teaspoons dried oregano
½ teaspoon salt
¼ teaspoon cayenne pepper
1½ pounds frozen cheese ravioli
½ cup chopped fresh parsley or basil

In a large saucepan, heat the oil over medium-high heat. Add the onion, bell pepper, garlic, and peppers. Cook, stirring, for 5 to 6 minutes. Stir in the tomato puree, stewed tomatoes, water, oregano, salt, and cayenne pepper, and bring to a simmer. Cook over medium-low heat for 15 to 20 minutes, stirring occasionally.

Meanwhile, in a large saucepan bring 4 quarts of water to a boil over medium-high heat. Place the ravioli in the boiling water, stir, and return to a boil. Cook until al dente, 9 to 11 minutes, stirring occasionally. Drain the ravioli in a colander.

Spoon the ravioli onto warm plates and ladle the sauce over each dish. Sprinkle with parsley or basil.

Makes 6 servings

Per Serving:
209 Calories; 10g Protein; 6g Fat; 19g Carbohydrates; 10mg Cholesterol; 443mg Sodium; 2g Fiber.

Artichoke Pilaf with Acini di Peppe and Black Beans

Rice and acini di peppe—tiny pasta tubes—make natural partners in this curry-flavored pilaf. Delicate artichokes and earthy black beans provide contrasting flavors and textures.

1 tablespoon canola oil
8 mushrooms, chopped
1 medium yellow onion, chopped
1 red bell pepper, seeded and diced
2 cloves garlic, minced
3 cups water
1¼ cups long-grain, white rice or parboiled rice
One 14-ounce can artichoke hearts, rinsed and coarsely chopped
½ cup acini di peppe
1 teaspoon curry powder
½ teaspoon salt
½ teaspoon freshly ground black pepper
1 cup cooked (or canned) and drained black beans
Juice of 2 lemons
¼ cup chopped fresh parsley

In a medium saucepan, heat the oil over medium-high heat. Add the mushrooms, onion, bell pepper, and garlic and cook, stirring, for 5 to 7 minutes.

Stir in the water and rice and bring to a simmer over high heat. Stir in the artichokes, acini di peppe, curry, salt, and pepper, and cover the pan. Cook over low heat until all of the liquid is absorbed, 15 to 20 minutes.

Remove the pan from the heat, fluff the grains with a fork, and fold in the black beans, lemon juice, and parsley. Let stand 5 to 10 minutes (still covered) before serving.

Makes 4 servings

VARIATION

Orzo may be substituted for acini di peppe.

Per Serving:
406 Calories; 13g Protein; 5g Fat; 78g Carbohydrates; 0 Cholesterol; 500mg Sodium; 7g Fiber.

Asian-Style Pasta Primavera

This soy-based primavera is a marriage of stir-fried vegetables and rice noodles. Feel free to improvise by adding bean sprouts, bamboo shoots, snow peas, or broccoli florets. Experiment with authoritative herbs, such as watercress, cilantro, or Thai basil when they're in season.

8 ounces rice or soba noodles
2 teaspoons peanut oil
1 red or yellow bell pepper, julienned
8 mushrooms, sliced
6 fresh shiitake mushrooms, halved (optional; see Helpful Hint)
2 teaspoons minced fresh gingerroot
10 small leaves of bok choy (see Helpful Hint) , cut into ribbons (chiffonade-style; see Helpful Hint, page 3)
4 whole scallions, trimmed and chopped
One 8-ounce can sliced water chestnuts, drained (see Helpful Hint)
4 ounces extra-firm tofu, cut into ¼-inch-wide matchsticks
½ cup vegetable broth
¼ cup low-sodium soy sauce
1 teaspoon sesame oil
1 tablespoon cornstarch
1 tablespoon water
¼ cup chopped roasted peanuts (preferably unsalted)

In a large saucepan, bring 3 quarts of water to a boil over medium-high heat. Place the noodles in the boiling water and cook until al dente, 4 to 5 minutes, stirring occasionally. Drain in a colander.

Meanwhile, in a large wok or skillet, heat the oil over medium-high heat. Add the bell pepper, mushrooms, and ginger. Cook, stirring, for 4 minutes. Stir in the bok choy, scallions, water chestnuts, and tofu and cook, stirring, for 3 to 4 minutes more. Stir in the vegetable broth, soy sauce, and sesame oil and bring to a simmer.

In a small mixing bowl, stir the cornstarch and water together until smooth. While continuing to stir, gradually drizzle the cornstarch paste into the vegetable mixture; return to a simmer. Fold in the cooked noodles.

Spoon the vegetables and noodles onto warm plates. Sprinkle the peanuts over the top and serve immediately.

Makes 4 servings

Per Serving:
417 Calories; 10g Protein; 13g Fat; 69g Carbohydrates; 0 Cholesterol; 747mg Sodium; 3g Fiber.

Helpful Hint

Shiitake mushrooms have a rubbery texture and deep woodsy flavor. Bok choy is a dark leafy green vegetable with a mild cabbagelike flavor. Water chestnuts are not nuts but rather the tubers of a water plant indigenous to Southeast Asia. All can be found in Asian markets and well-stocked supermarkets.

Fettuccine with Creamy Avocado Sauce

Fettuccine noodles are adorned with a velvety sauce of pureed avocados, tomatoes, and a hint of lime. The sauce has the texture of an Alfredo sauce, minus the cream, butter, cheese, and eggs. With the aid of a blender, the uncooked sauce can be prepared in the time it takes to make the pasta.

3 large ripe tomatoes, diced
2 ripe avocados, peeled, pitted
and diced
¼ cup chopped red onion
2 cloves garlic, minced
1 hot chili pepper, seeded and
minced (optional)
Juice of 1 large lime
2 tablespoons chopped fresh
cilantro
1 teaspoon ground cumin
1 teaspoon salt
½ teaspoon freshly ground
black pepper
12 ounces fettuccine
2 scallions, chopped

Combine the tomatoes, avocados, onion, garlic, chili pepper (if desired), lime juice, cilantro, cumin, salt, and pepper in a blender or food processor fitted with a steel blade. Process until liquefied, 5 to 10 seconds. Set aside until the pasta is ready.

In a large saucepan, bring 4 quarts of water to a boil over medium-high heat. Place the fettuccine in the boiling water, stir, and return to a boil. Cook until al dente, 8 to 10 minutes, stirring occasionally. Drain in a colander.

Transfer the pasta to warm serving plates and ladle the avocado sauce over the top. Sprinkle with scallions and serve at once.

Makes 6 servings

VARIATION

Before adding the sauce to the pasta, toss in seasonal vegetables such as steamed broccoli, green beans, asparagus, or braised greens.

Per Serving:
290 Calories; 7g Protein; 10g Fat; 46g Carbohydrates; 0 Cholesterol; 400mg Sodium; 9g Fiber.

Curried Squash and Pasta Soup

Pasta adds sustenance to this broth of winter vegetables and curry spices.
A dollop of yogurt offers a soothing contrast to the warm curry flavors.

1 tablespoon canola oil
1 large yellow onion, diced
1 stalk celery, diced
1 large tomato, diced
4 cloves garlic, minced
2 teaspoons curry powder
1 teaspoon ground cumin
½ teaspoon garam masala
    (optional; see Helpful Hint)
1 teaspoon salt
½ teaspoon freshly ground
    black pepper
6 cups vegetable broth or
    water
2 cups peeled, diced butternut
    squash
1 large carrot, diced
½ cup conchiglie or ditalini
¼ cup chopped fresh parsley
½ cup low-fat, plain yogurt

In a large saucepan, heat the oil over medium-high heat. Add the onion and celery and cook, stirring, for 4 minutes. Add the tomato and garlic, and cook, stirring, for 3 minutes more. Stir in the curry, cumin, garam masala (if desired), salt and pepper, and cook, stirring, for 1 minute more over low heat.

Add the broth or water, squash, and carrot, and bring to a simmer over high heat. Reduce heat to medium and cook, stirring occasionally, until the squash is tender, about 15 minutes.

Stir in the pasta and parsley and return to a simmer. Cook over medium heat until the pasta is al dente, about 10 minutes. Remove from the heat and let stand for 5 minutes before serving.

Pour the soup into serving bowls and spoon a dollop of yogurt over the top of each serving.

Makes 6 servings

Per Serving:
138 Calories; 6g Protein; 4g Fat; 24g Carbohydrates; 1mg Cholesterol; 1,417mg Sodium; 2g Fiber.

Helpful Hint

Garam masala is a blend of dry, roasted Indian spices, such as cumin, coriander, chili peppers, and others. It is sold in Indian groceries and in some supermarkets.

Solstice Pasta with Lemon-Scented Vegetables

*This light, summery dish is spartan when it comes to calories—
but radiant with pleasure when it comes to flavor.*

**6 ripe tomatoes, coarsely
    chopped**
**One 14-ounce can artichoke
    hearts, drained and
    coarsely chopped**
**2 cups cooked corn kernels
    (preferably fresh)**
**4 scallions, trimmed and
    chopped**
**¼ cup chopped basil
    (chiffonade-style; see
    Helpful Hints, page 3)**
¼ cup chopped fresh parsley
2 cloves garlic, minced
2 tablespoons olive oil
**½ teaspoon freshly ground
    black pepper**
½ teaspoon salt
Juice of 2 lemons
8 ounces penne or ziti

Place the chopped tomatoes in a colander and let drain for about 1 minute, stirring at least once. Transfer the tomatoes to a large serving bowl and combine with all of the remaining ingredients, except the pasta. Let stand at room temperature until the pasta is ready.

In a large saucepan, bring 3 quarts of water to a boil over medium-high heat. Place the penne or ziti in the boiling water, stir, and return to a boil. Cook until al dente, 9 to 11 minutes, stirring occasionally. Drain the pasta in a colander.

Fold the pasta into the tomato-corn mixture. Serve at once.

Makes 6 servings

Per Serving:
256 Calories; 8g Protein; 6g Fat;
46g Carbohydrates; 0 Cholesterol;
372mg Sodium; 5g Fiber.

Pasta with Market Vegetable Ragout

The simplicity of this rustic tomato sauce is almost too good to be true. Fresh vegetables and herbs are simmered to a chunky ragoutlike consistency and then ladled over the pasta. Paprika gives the sauce a reddish-orange hue.

2 teaspoons canola oil
1 medium zucchini, halved lengthwise and thinly cut diagonally
1 red or green bell pepper, julienned
2 cups diced eggplant
4 cloves garlic, minced
1 hot chili pepper, seeded and minced (optional)
4 large tomatoes, diced
½ cup chopped mixed fresh herbs (purple basil, sweet basil, or parsley)
1 teaspoon dried oregano
1 teaspoon paprika
½ teaspoon freshly ground black pepper
½ teaspoon salt
8 ounces capellini or spaghetti
¼ cup freshly grated Parmesan or Romano cheese (optional)

In a large skillet or wok, heat the oil over medium-high heat. Add the zucchini, bell pepper, eggplant, garlic, and chili pepper (if desired). Cook, stirring, for 7 to 9 minutes. Add the tomatoes, herbs, oregano, paprika, pepper, and salt, and cook for 10 minutes more over medium heat, stirring occasionally. As the tomatoes "cook down," the mixture will thicken.

Meanwhile, in a large saucepan, bring 3 quarts of water to a boil over medium-high heat. Place the pasta in the boiling water, stir, and return to a boil. Cook until al dente, 4 to 6 minutes, stirring occasionally, if using capellini, 9 to 11 minutes if using spaghetti. Drain in a colander.

Transfer the pasta to warm serving dishes. Spoon the vegetable sauce over the top; sprinkle with Parmesan cheese if desired. Serve with warm bread.

Makes 4 servings

Per Serving:
253 Calories; 8g Protein; 4g Fat; 50g Carbohydrates; 0 Cholesterol; 312mg Sodium; 5g Fiber.

Gnocchi with Ricotta Pesto

This combination of creamy pesto and chewy potato gnocchi is a match made in pasta heaven. Ricotta pesto is lighter than traditional oil-based pesto but just as fragrant and alluring.

4 to 6 cloves garlic, coarsely chopped
½ cup diced walnuts
2 ripe tomatoes, diced
2 cups coarsely chopped spinach
1 cup basil leaves, coarsely chopped
1 cup part-skim ricotta cheese
½ teaspoon salt
½ teaspoon freshly ground black pepper
1½ pounds frozen gnocchi

In a blender or food processor fitted with a steel blade, add the garlic, walnuts, and tomatoes, and process until pureed, 5 to 10 seconds, stopping once to scrape the sides. With the machine off, fold in the spinach, basil, ricotta, salt, and pepper. Process until liquefied, 5 to 10 seconds more, stopping again to scrape the sides and fold the mixture. Set aside until the gnocchi is ready.

Meanwhile, in a large saucepan, bring 4 quarts of water to a boil over medium-high heat. Place the gnocchi in the boiling water, stir, and return to a boil. Cook until al dente, 4 to 5 minutes, stirring occasionally. Drain in a colander.

Transfer the gnocchi to a large serving bowl and ladle the pesto over the top. Fold the pasta and gnocchi together and serve at once. Any leftovers can be served as a salad the next day.

Makes 6 servings

VARIATIONS

A variety of ingredients can be tossed with the pasta, such as steamed broccoli florets, green beans, artichoke hearts, chickpeas, or roasted bell peppers.

If gnocchi is unavailable, substitute 1 pound of dried pasta such as orecchiette or cavatelli.

Per Serving:
271 Calories; 12g Protein; 8g Fat; 36g Carbohydrates; 6mg Cholesterol; 233mg Sodium; 6g Fiber.

Beet Fettuccine with Horseradish Tomato Sauce

*Although pungent horseradish is not a common ingredient in pasta
dishes, it does have potential when used with discretion. Horseradish
is often served with beets, so pairing this sauce with beet-flavored
pasta seems like a natural.*

1 tablespoon olive oil
1 medium yellow onion, diced
2 or 3 cloves garlic, minced
**One 28-ounce can plum
  tomatoes**
**2 cups coarsely chopped
  spinach**
**1 tablespoon prepared
  horseradish**
1 tablespoon dried parsley
1 teaspoon dried basil
**½ teaspoon freshly ground
  black pepper**
½ teaspoon salt
**12 ounces beet or spinach
  fettuccine**

In a large saucepan, heat the oil over medium-high heat. Add the onion and garlic and cook, stirring, for 4 minutes. Stir in the plum tomatoes, spinach, horseradish, parsley, basil, pepper, and salt, and bring to a simmer. Reduce the heat to low and cook for 15 minutes, stirring occasionally.

Transfer the sauce to a blender or a food processor fitted with a steel blade and process until smooth, 5 to 10 seconds. Keep warm until the fettuccine is ready.

Meanwhile, in another large saucepan, bring 4 quarts of water to a boil over medium-high heat. Place the fettuccine in the boiling water, stir, and return to a boil. Cook until al dente, 4 to 6 minutes, stirring occasionally. Drain in a colander.

When the sauce is ready, transfer the pasta to warm serving plates and spoon the sauce over the top.

Makes 6 servings

Per Serving:
265 Calories; 11g Protein; 5g Fat;
43g Carbohydrates; 68mg Cholesterol; 637mg Sodium; 6g Fiber.

Spaghetti with Garden Tomato Sauce

This sauce highlights the powerful allure of ripe garden tomatoes. Chunks of tofu or seitan, a meatlike food made from wheat gluten, add a chewy substance to the sauce. Hey, who needs meatballs?

8 large ripe tomatoes, coarsely chopped
2 tablespoons olive oil
1 medium red onion, chopped
4 cloves garlic, minced
1 teaspoon salt
½ teaspoon freshly ground black pepper
8 ounces extra-firm tofu or seitan, diced (see Helpful Hint)
¼ cup chopped fresh basil
¼ cup chopped fresh parsley
2 teaspoons honey
12 ounces spaghetti
¼ cup freshly grated Parmesan cheese (optional)

Place the chopped tomatoes in a colander and let drain for about 1 minute. Stir the tomatoes once or twice with a large spoon.

In a large saucepan, heat the oil over medium-high heat. Add the onion and garlic and cook, stirring, for 3 minutes. Add the tomatoes, salt, and pepper, and cook over medium heat, stirring occasionally, until the tomatoes

become thick and saucelike, 15 to 20 minutes. Let cool slightly.

Transfer the tomato mixture to a blender and process until smooth, about 10 seconds. Return the sauce to the pan and stir in the tofu or seitan, basil, parsley, and honey. Bring back to a gentle simmer.

Meanwhile, in a large saucepan, bring 3 quarts of water to a boil over medium-high heat. Place the spaghetti in the boiling water, stir, and return to a boil. Cook until al dente, 9 to 11 minutes, stirring occasionally. Drain the spaghetti in a colander and shake well.

Transfer the spaghetti to a large serving dish. Ladle the sauce over the cooked pasta. If desired, offer grated Parmesan cheese as a garnish.

Makes 4 servings

Helpful Hint

Seitan is a chewy, high-protein meat substitute made from the gluten of whole wheat flour. It is sold as either a dry mix or as ready-prepared in the refrigerated section of natural food stores.

Per Serving:
400 Calories; 17g Protein; 9g Fat; 67g Carbohydrates; 0 Cholesterol; 615mg Sodium; 7g Fiber.

Lemon-Tossed Pasta with Sautéed Garden Vegetables

Tangy lemons are valuable assets in the low-fat kitchen. The citrus fruit perks up this light pasta dish of penne, basil, and sautéed vegetables.

12 ounces penne (see Helpful Hints)
1 tablespoon olive oil
1 medium zucchini, halved lengthwise and thinly cut diagonally
1 red or green bell pepper, seeded and julienned
10 to 12 mushrooms, sliced
2 cloves garlic, minced
2 large tomatoes, diced
½ cup coarsely chopped fresh basil (see Helpful Hints)
¼ cup freshly grated Parmesan or Romano cheese (optional)
½ teaspoon freshly ground black pepper
½ teaspoon salt
2 lemons, quartered

In a large saucepan, bring 3 quarts of water to a boil over medium-high heat. Place the pasta in the boiling water, stir, and return to a boil. Cook, stirring occasionally, until al dente, 9 to 11 minutes. Drain in a colander.

Meanwhile, in a large skillet or wok, heat the oil over medium-high heat. Add the zucchini, bell pepper, mushrooms, and garlic and cook, stirring, for 5 minutes. Add the tomatoes and cook over medium heat for about 7 minutes more, stirring frequently.

In a large serving bowl, combine the penne, vegetables, basil, cheese (if desired), pepper, and salt. Squeeze 1 lemon over the pasta and toss again before serving. Pass the extra lemon wedges at the table.

Makes 4 servings

Helpful Hints

Flavored pasta (such as parsley-garlic or spinach penne) also works well.

If fresh basil is unavailable, try ½ cup chopped arugula or parsley.

Per Serving:
190 Calories; 7g Protein; 5g Fat; 32g Carbohydrates; 0 Cholesterol; 311mg Sodium; 2g Fiber.

Arrabiata Spaghetti with Mushrooms and Peppers

This piquant Italian dish is seasoned with red pepper flakes and feisty pepperoncinis (yellowish-green Italian hot peppers). Arrabiata means "enraged" or "angry" in Italian. Pepperoncinis can be found in the Italian section of most supermarkets.

2 tablespoons olive oil
12 ounces mushrooms, sliced
1 green bell pepper, seeded and
    julienned
2 or 3 cloves garlic, minced
One 14-ounce can stewed
    tomatoes
One 14-ounce can tomato puree
2 or 3 pepperoncinis, seeded
    and minced
2 teaspoons dried oregano
1 teaspoon dried basil
½ teaspoon red pepper flakes
½ teaspoon salt
12 ounces spaghetti

In a large saucepan, heat the oil over high heat. Add the mushrooms, bell pepper, and garlic and cook, stirring, over medium heat for 7 to 9 minutes. Stir in the stewed tomatoes, tomato puree, pepperoncinis, oregano, basil, red pepper flakes, and salt. Reduce the heat to low and cook for 20 minutes, stirring occasionally.

Meanwhile, in another large saucepan bring 3 quarts of water to a boil over medium-high heat. Place the spaghetti in the boiling water, stir, and return to a boil. Cook until al dente, stirring occasionally, 8 to 10 minutes. Drain the spaghetti in a colander.

When the sauce is ready, transfer the spaghetti to warm serving plates and spoon the sauce over the top. Serve with warm Italian bread.

Makes 4 servings

VARIATION

For an even spicier dish, add one or two fresh jalapeño or serrano peppers (seeded and minced) to the sauce along with the mushrooms and pepper.

Per Serving:
476 Calories; 15g Protein; 9g Fat;
87g Carbohydrates; 0 Cholesterol;
1,000mg Sodium; 9g Fiber.

Risotto with Orzo and Butternut Squash

For this savory twist on the creamy Italian rice dish, rice-shaped orzo teams up splendidly with arborio rice. Orzo also adds substance to the dish while "extending" the more expensive Italian grain. Butternut squash melds seamlessly into the pot.

2 tablespoons olive oil
10 to 12 mushrooms, sliced
1 medium yellow onion, finely chopped
4 cloves garlic, minced
2 cups butternut squash, peeled and diced
1 cup arborio rice (see Helpful Hint)
½ cup orzo
5 cups water
½ teaspoon white pepper
½ teaspoon salt
½ teaspoon turmeric
1 cup green peas, fresh or frozen
⅓ to ½ cup freshly grated Romano cheese

In a large saucepan, heat the oil over medium heat. Add the mushrooms, onion, and garlic, and cook, stirring, for 5 to 6 minutes. Stir in the squash, rice, orzo, 3 cups water, pepper, salt, and turmeric. Cook uncovered over medium heat for 10 minutes, stirring frequently.

Gradually stir in the remaining 2 cups water and the peas and cook, stirring, until the rice and squash are tender, 12 to 15 minutes more.

Remove from the heat and fold in the cheese. Let stand for about 5 minutes before serving.

Makes 4 servings

Helpful Hint

Arborio rice is a short-grained rice available in either the Italian section or the grain section of well-stocked supermarkets. Valencia rice is sometimes substituted.

Per Serving:
434 Calories; 12g Protein; 10g Fat; 74g Carbohydrates; 8mg Cholesterol; 445mg Sodium; 4g Fiber.

Javanese Rice Noodles with Lime-Peanut Sauce

The quartet of peanut butter, soy sauce, ginger, and lime form the foundation of myriad Southeast Asian sauces. The nutty-and-sour sauce is nicely balanced by the mildly flavored rice noodles.

2 teaspoons peanut oil
1 cup snow peas, trimmed and coarsely chopped
1 tablespoon minced fresh gingerroot
1 jalapeño or serrano chili pepper, seeded and minced
½ pound extra-firm tofu, cut into ¼-inch-wide matchsticks
4 scallions, trimmed and chopped
½ cup roasted sweet bell peppers, diced
¼ cup chunky peanut butter
¼ cup vegetable broth
¼ cup low-sodium soy sauce
1½ teaspoons dark or "toasted" sesame oil
Juice of 1 large lime
2 or 3 tablespoons chopped cilantro
8 ounces rice vermicelli

In a large wok or skillet, heat the oil over medium-high heat. Add the snow peas, ginger, and chili pepper and cook, stirring, for 2 minutes. Add the tofu, scallions, and roasted peppers and cook, stirring, for 3 minutes more. Reduce the heat to low and whisk in the peanut butter, broth, soy sauce, sesame oil, lime juice, and cilantro. Remove from the heat and let stand until the vermicelli is ready.

Meanwhile, in a large saucepan bring 3 quarts of water to a boil. Place the vermicelli in the boiling water, stir, and turn off the heat. Let the noodles steep until al dente, about 5 minutes, stirring occasionally. Drain the vermicelli in a colander and fold into the peanut-lime dressing. Serve immediately.

Makes 4 servings

Per Serving:
428 Calories; 17g Protein; 12g Fat; 56g Carbohydrates; 0 Cholesterol; 629mg Sodium; 7g Fiber.

Sopa de Fideo (Mexican Corn Noodle Soup)

This authentic Mexican soup beckons with colorful vegetables, assertive spices, and piquant tastes. The presence of gourmet spaghetti (either corn or wheat) gives the humble dish a sophisticated allure.

1 tablespoon canola oil
2 large carrots, diced
1 medium yellow onion, diced
1 red or green bell pepper,
    seeded and diced
2 or 3 cloves garlic, minced
1 jalapeño or serrano chili
    pepper, seeded and minced
Two 14½-ounce cans vegetable
    broth
1 cup water
2 tablespoons tomato paste
2 teaspoons dried oregano
1 teaspoon ground cumin
½ teaspoon freshly ground
    black pepper
4 ounces corn spaghetti or
    whole wheat spaghetti,
    snapped in half
1 cup cooked (or canned) and
    drained red kidney beans

In a large saucepan, heat the oil over medium-high heat. Add the carrots, onion, bell pepper, garlic, and chili pepper and cook, stirring, for 7 minutes. Add the broth, water, tomato paste, oregano, cumin, and pepper, and bring to a simmer over high heat, stirring occasionally. Stir in the spaghetti and beans and return to simmer.

Reduce the heat to medium-high and cook, stirring occasionally, until the spaghetti is al dente, 8 to 12 minutes. Remove from the heat and let stand for a few minutes before serving.

Ladle the soup into shallow bowls and serve with warmed flour tortillas.

Makes 4 servings

Helpful Hint

For an herbal nuance, add 2 or 3 tablespoons chopped cilantro to the soup minutes before serving.

Per Serving:
211 Calories; 7g Protein; 4g Fat;
36g Carbohydrates; 0 Cholesterol;
58mg Sodium; 6g Fiber.

Gnocchi Ratatouille Stew

Gnocchi, a "potato" pasta, makes a hearty addition to soups and stews. For this dish, gnocchi enlivens the classic Mediterranean eggplant stew. Despite their dumplinglike shape, the frozen gnocchi cook up quickly (in about five minutes).

12 ounces frozen gnocchi
1 to 2 tablespoons canola oil
1 medium yellow onion, diced
1 green bell pepper, seeded and
diced
8 ounces mushrooms, sliced
2 cups diced eggplant
4 cloves garlic, minced
One 14-ounce can stewed
tomatoes
One 14-ounce can crushed
tomatoes or tomato puree
1 tablespoon dried parsley
2 teaspoons dried oregano
½ teaspoon freshly ground
black pepper
½ teaspoon salt
¼ cup chopped fresh basil
(optional)

In a large saucepan, bring 4 quarts of water to a boil over medium-high heat. Place the gnocchi in the boiling water, stir, and return to a boil. Cook until al dente, about 5 minutes. Drain in a colander.

Meanwhile, in another large saucepan, heat the oil over medium heat. Add the onion, bell pepper, mushrooms, eggplant, and garlic and cook, stirring, until the vegetables are tender, 8 to 10 minutes. Stir in the stewed and crushed tomatoes, parsley, and oregano; cook over medium-low heat for 15 minutes, stirring occasionally.

Remove from the heat and stir in the cooked gnocchi and basil (if desired). Ladle the ratatouille in shallow bowls and serve warm Italian bread on the side.

Makes 4 servings

Per Serving:
251 Calories; 6g Protein; 10g Fat; 37g Carbohydrates; 16mg Cholesterol; 595mg Sodium; 5g Fiber.

Wheat Spaghetti with Lemon-Braised Broccoli Rabe

Also called rapini, broccoli rabe is a leafy green with miniature broccoli florets. It has an assertive, almost strident, mustardy flavor similar to turnip greens.

1 large bunch broccoli rabe (rapini)
2 teaspoons olive oil or canola oil
3 cloves garlic, minced
½ teaspoon freshly ground black pepper
½ teaspoon salt
Juice of 2 lemons
8 ounces whole wheat or spelt spaghetti
¼ cup freshly grated Asiago or other strong Parmesan cheese

Remove the fibrous stems of the broccoli rabe and discard. Rinse and coarsely chop the leaves.

In a large, wide skillet, heat the oil over medium heat. Add the garlic and cook, stirring, for 2 minutes. Stir in the broccoli rabe, pepper, salt, and lemon juice. Cook, stirring frequently, until the greens are wilted and tender, 5 to 6 minutes.

Meanwhile, in a large saucepan, bring 3 quarts of water to a boil over medium-high heat. Place the spaghetti in the boiling water, stir, and return to a boil. Cook until al dente, stirring occasionally, 8 to 10 minutes. Drain in a colander.

Transfer the pasta to a large serving bowl. Add the broccoli rabe mixture and toss together with the pasta. Lightly sprinkle the Parmesan cheese over the top. Serve immediately.

Makes 4 servings

Per Serving:
248 Calories; 12g Protein; 5g Fat; 44g Carbohydrates; 4mg Cholesterol; 409mg Sodium; 9g Fiber.

Wheat Pasta al Pomodoro with Artichokes and Arugula

This sauce reflects the Italian tradition of using leftover bread in soups and red sauces. It is also an economical way to add body to a sauce with minimum fat and calories.

3 slices firm dark bread or Italian bread
1 tablespoon olive oil
1 medium yellow onion, diced
3 or 4 cloves garlic, minced
One 28-ounce can plum tomatoes
2 teaspoons dried oregano
2 teaspoons dried parsley
½ teaspoon salt
½ teaspoon freshly ground black pepper
One 14-ounce can artichoke hearts, drained and coarsely chopped
2 cups coarsely chopped arugula (see Helpful Hint)
4 ounces extra-firm tofu, diced
8 ounces whole wheat spaghetti or linguine

Lightly toast the bread in a toaster (or in a preheated oven at 300°F). Cut the bread into croutonlike cubes. (There should be about 2 cups.)

In a large saucepan, heat the oil over medium-high heat. Add the onion and garlic and cook, stirring, for 3 to 4 minutes. Stir in the plum tomatoes, oregano, parsley, salt, pepper, and cubed bread, and bring to a simmer. Cook for about 15 minutes over medium-low heat, stirring occasionally.

Remove from the heat and transfer to a blender or a food processor fitted with a steel blade; puree. Return the sauce to the pan, add the artichokes, arugula, and tofu, and return to a gentle simmer over medium-low heat. Cook, stirring, for 5 to 7 minutes.

Meanwhile, in another large saucepan, bring 3 quarts of water to a boil over medium-high heat. Place spaghetti or linguine in boiling water, stir, and return to a boil. Cook until al dente, stirring occasionally, 8 to 10 minutes. Drain in a colander.

Transfer the pasta to warm serving plates. Ladle the sauce over the top.

Makes 4 servings

Per Serving:
400 Calories; 19g Protein; 7g Fat; 66g Carbohydrates; 0 Cholesterol; 1,078mg Sodium; 11g Fiber.

Helpful Hint

Arugula is a pale green leafy herb with a peppery flavor. It can be found in well-stocked supermarkets throughout the year but is widely available in spring and autumn. If arugula is not available, spinach may be substituted.

Spinach Pasta with Mint Pesto and Summer Vegetables

This versatile meal can be served as a hot entrée or as a chilled salad course.

8 ounces spinach rotini or penne
1 tablespoon canola oil
1 medium yellow squash, halved lengthwise and thinly sliced diagonally
1 red bell pepper, seeded and cut into thin strips
4 ounces snow peas, trimmed and halved
4 ounces extra-firm tofu, cut into ¼-inch-wide strips
1 cup Mint Pesto (page 171) or your favorite commercial pesto

In a large saucepan, bring 2½ quarts of water to a boil over medium-high heat. Place the pasta in the boiling water, stir, and return to a boil. Cook until al dente, stirring occasionally, 10 to 12 minutes. Drain in a colander.

Meanwhile, in a large skillet or wok, heat the oil over high heat. Add the squash, bell pepper, and snow peas and cook, stirring, for 4 minutes. Add the tofu and cook, stirring, for 4 minutes more.

In a large serving bowl, combine vegetable-tofu mixture and pesto. Fold in the pasta. Serve immediately as an entrée or refrigerate and serve later as a chilled salad.

Makes 6 servings

Per Serving:
231 Calories; 10g Protein; 13g Fat; 16g Carbohydrates; 9mg Cholesterol; 211mg Sodium; 6g Fiber.

Spaghetti Western

Robustly flavored sun-dried tomatoes and luscious avocados add a decadent twist to this simple but inventive gourmet pasta dish. This is an opportunity to try out a specialty spaghetti made from spelt, quinoa, or whole wheat.

8 ounces whole grain spaghetti (spelt, quinoa, or whole wheat)

3 ounces sun-dried tomatoes (not oil-packed variety)

2 large cloves garlic, minced

4 ounces tofu, cut into ¼-inch-wide strips

1 ripe avocado, peeled, pitted, and cubed

4 ounces mozzarella, cut into ¼-inch-wide strips or 2 ounces goat cheese (optional)

½ cup roasted red bell pepper, diced

¼ cup chopped fresh parsley

1 to 2 tablespoons olive oil

½ teaspoon freshly ground black pepper

½ teaspoon salt

In a large saucepan, bring 3 quarts of water to a boil over medium-high heat. Place the spaghetti in the boiling water, stir, and return to a boil. Cook until al dente, stirring occasionally, for 5 to 8 minutes (depending on the variety). Drain in a colander.

Meanwhile, in a medium saucepan, bring 1 quart of water to a boil. Place the sun-dried tomatoes in the boiling water and cook for 2 minutes. Drain the tomatoes in a colander and coarsely chop.

Transfer the pasta to a large serving bowl. Add the sun-dried tomatoes and remaining ingredients and toss together. Let the pasta stand for a few minutes to allow the flavors to meld.

Makes 4 servings

Per Serving:
337 Calories; 15g Protein; 10g Fat; 43g Carbohydrates; 0 Cholesterol; 180mg Sodium; 6g Fiber.

Capellini with Almonds and Julienned Yellow Squash

Capellini, also called angel-hair pasta, are delicate strands of pasta that cook up in minutes. The thin noodles are paired with light herbs, nutty almonds, and thinly sliced zucchini.

8 ounces capellini (angel-hair pasta)
1 to 2 tablespoons olive oil
1 zucchini, halved crosswise and cut into ¼-inch-wide strips
1 yellow squash or another zucchini, halved crosswise and cut into ¼-inch-wide strips
1 medium red onion, cut into thin slivers
1 teaspoon dried oregano
1 teaspoon dried basil
½ teaspoon freshly ground black pepper
½ teaspoon salt
¼ cup slivered almonds
2 lemons, quartered

In a large saucepan, bring 3 quarts of water to a boil over medium-high heat. Place the pasta in the boiling water, stir, and return to a boil. Cook until al dente, stirring occasionally, 3 to 4 minutes. Drain in a colander.

Meanwhile, in a large skillet or wok, heat the oil over medium-high heat. Add the zucchini, yellow squash, and onion and cook, stirring, for 5 minutes. Stir in the oregano, basil, pepper, salt, and almonds, and cook for 30 seconds more. Remove the pan from the heat and squeeze one of the lemons over the vegetables.

Add the cooked pasta to the vegetables and toss thoroughly. Serve in a large serving bowl and garnish with the remaining lemon wedges.

Makes 4 servings

Per Serving:
264 Calories; 8g Protein; 9g Fat; 41g Carbohydrates; 0 Cholesterol; 297mg Sodium; 5g Fiber.

Rigatoni with Chunky Eggplant and Black Bean Ragout

Rigatoni is a large, tubular-shaped pasta that demands a sturdy, earthy sauce. This hearty eggplant and bean ragout fills the bill admirably.

2 tablespoons dry red wine
1 tablespoon olive oil
1 medium yellow onion, diced
2 cups diced eggplant
1 small zucchini, diced
2 cloves garlic, minced
One 28-ounce can stewed or plum tomatoes
One 15-ounce can black beans, drained
2 teaspoons dried oregano
2 teaspoons dried basil
½ teaspoon salt
¼ teaspoon red pepper flakes
8 ounces rigatoni
¼ cup freshly grated Parmesan cheese (optional)

In a large saucepan, heat the wine and oil over medium-high heat. Add the onion, eggplant, zucchini, and garlic and cook, stirring, for about 8 minutes. Add the tomatoes, beans, oregano, basil, salt, and red pepper flakes and bring to a simmer. Cook for 15 minutes over medium-low heat, stirring occasionally. As it cooks, break up the tomatoes into small chunks with a spoon.

Meanwhile, in a large saucepan, bring 3 quarts of water to a boil over medium-high heat. Place the rigatoni in the boiling water, stir, and return to a boil. Cook until al dente, stirring occasionally, 13 to 15 minutes. Drain in a colander.

Place the rigatoni in a large shallow bowl and ladle the ragout over the top. If desired, sprinkle with Parmesan cheese. Serve at once.

Makes 4 servings

Per Serving:
349 Calories; 12g Protein; 5g Fat; 71g Carbohydrates; 0 Cholesterol; 1,243mg Sodium; 12g Fiber.

Rotelle with Brazilian Black Beans and Hearts of Palm

The playful shape of rotelle (wagon wheel pasta) makes it a natural staple for inventive, offbeat dishes. This creation combines three of Brazil's cherished staples: hearts of palm, kale, and black beans.

1 tablespoon olive oil
1 medium yellow onion, diced
1 sweet bell pepper, seeded and diced
2 cloves garlic, minced
One 28-ounce can crushed tomatoes
One 15-ounce can black beans, drained
2 cups coarsely chopped kale or green chard
2 tablespoons dry red wine
2 teaspoons dried oregano
½ teaspoon salt
½ teaspoon freshly ground black pepper
14½-ounce can hearts of palm, rinsed and cut into 1-inch pieces (see Helpful Hint)
12 ounces rotelle (wagon wheel pasta)
¼ cup chopped fresh parsley

In a large saucepan, heat the oil over medium-high heat. Add the onion, bell pepper, and garlic and cook, stirring, for about 6 minutes. Add the tomatoes, beans, kale or chard, wine, oregano, salt, and pepper, and bring to a simmer. Cook for 15 minutes over medium-low heat, stirring occasionally. Stir in the hearts of palm.

Meanwhile, in another large saucepan, bring 4 quarts of water to a boil over medium-high heat. Place the rotelle in the boiling water, stir, and return to a boil. Cook until al dente, stirring occasionally, 8 to 10 minutes. Drain in a colander.

Place the rotelle in a large shallow serving bowl. Ladle the sauce over the top, sprinkle with parsley, and serve at once.

Makes 4 servings

Helpful Hint

Hearts of palm are the interior edible portions of the cabbage palm tree. They resemble white asparagus without the tips. They are available plain or marinated in the canned vegetable section of most supermarkets. (Look for them alongside canned artichokes.)

Per Serving:
522 Calories; 20g Protein; 6g Fat; 104g Carbohydrates; 0 Cholesterol; 370mg Sodium; 13g Fiber.

Middle Eastern Roasted Noodle Pilaf

For this classic Middle Eastern dish, noodles are combined with rice, vegetables, and chickpeas for a nourishing one-pot meal. The pasta is quickly "roasted" in a skillet beforehand, a process that yields a toasty flavor.

6 ounces capellini or vermicelli
1 tablespoon canola oil
1 tablespoon olive oil
1 medium yellow onion, chopped
1 red bell pepper, seeded and diced
3½ cups vegetable broth or water
1¼ cups long-grain, brown rice
2 carrots, diced
½ teaspoon turmeric
½ teaspoon freshly ground black pepper
½ teaspoon ground cumin
½ teaspoon salt
One 15-ounce can chickpeas, drained

Break the capellini into small pieces about ½ to 1 inch long. (This can be done over a large bowl with your hands.)

To roast the noodles, heat the canola oil in a large skillet over medium heat. Add the noodles and cook, stirring, until the noodles are golden brown, 4 to 5 minutes. Remove the pan from the heat; set aside.

Meanwhile, in another large saucepan, heat the olive oil. Add the onion and bell pepper and cook, stirring, for 4 to 5 minutes. Stir in the broth or water, rice, carrots, turmeric, pepper, cumin, and salt, and bring to a simmer over high heat. Cover the pan, reduce the heat to low, and cook for 10 minutes.

Stir in the roasted noodles and chickpeas, cover, and cook until all of the liquid is absorbed, 20 to 25 minutes, stirring at least once.

Remove the pilaf from the heat and fluff the grains and noodles with a fork. Let stand for 5 to 10 minutes before serving.

Makes 4 servings

Per Serving:
380 Calories; 13g Protein; 10g Fat; 63g Carbohydrates; 0 Cholesterol; 1,480mg Sodium; 8g Fiber.

Buckwheat "Noodle Shop" Miso Soup

Miso is a naturally low-fat paste made of fermented soy beans and grains, used in Asian cuisine as a seasoning or condiment. It contributes a mild, sea-salt flavor to this traditional, Japanese-style soup.

2 teaspoons peanut oil
2 carrots, peeled and thinly sliced at an angle
2 cloves garlic, minced
1 teaspoon minced fresh gingerroot
5 cups vegetable broth
2 cups coarsely chopped bok choy leaves
¼ pound extra-firm tofu, diced
One 2-inch section of daikon or 2 radishes, thinly sliced (see Helpful Hints)
2 to 3 tablespoons low-sodium soy sauce (or shoyu sauce; see Helpful Hints)
½ teaspoon freshly ground black pepper
8 ounces soba or udon noodles
2 tablespoons miso (see Helpful Hints)
2 scallions, trimmed and chopped

In a large saucepan, heat the oil over medium-high heat. Add the carrots, garlic, and ginger and cook, stirring, for 2 minutes. Add the broth, bok choy, tofu, daikon or radishes, soy sauce or shoyu, and black pepper and bring to a simmer. Cook over medium heat for about 10 minutes, stirring occasionally.

In another large saucepan, bring 3 quarts of water to a boil over medium-high heat. Place the noodles in the boiling water, stir, and return to a boil. Cook until al dente, stirring occasionally, 6 to 8 minutes. Drain the noodles in a colander.

Meanwhile, in a cup, dissolve the miso in 2 to 3 tablespoons warm water. During the last minute of cooking, stir the miso mixture into the broth mixture, and cook for about 1 minute more. Do not boil once the miso has been added.

Serve the cooked noodles in large soup bowls. Ladle the miso broth over the noodles. Sprinkle the scallions over the top.

Makes 4 to 6 servings

Per Serving:
319 Calories; 14g Protein; 5g Fat; 56g Carbohydrates; 0 Cholesterol; 1,219mg Sodium; 5g Fiber.

Helpful Hints

Daikon is a large, white, rootlike radish with a mild degree of sharpness. It is available in Japanese groceries and some supermarkets.

Shoyu is a variety of Japanese soy sauce.

Miso comes in a variety of flavors, including barley (also called red), rice (white), and soy (dark). Darker varieties are stronger in flavor. Miso can be purchased at natural food stores.

Penne with Wild Mushroom Sauce

The availability of wild mushrooms has skyrocketed in recent years. A mélange of mushrooms brings a woodsy flavor and chunky texture to this hearty dish.

2 tablespoons olive oil
8 ounces button mushrooms, sliced
6 ounces cremini (Italian brown) mushrooms, sliced (see Helpful Hints)
4 ounces fresh oyster or shiitake mushrooms, sliced (see Helpful Hints)
4 cloves garlic, minced
One 14-ounce can stewed tomatoes
One 14-ounce can tomato puree
¼ cup water
2 teaspoons dried oregano
1 teaspoon dried basil
½ teaspoon freshly ground black pepper
½ teaspoon salt
¼ cup fresh basil leaves, coarsely chopped
12 ounces penne

In a large saucepan, heat the oil over medium heat. Add the mushrooms and garlic and cook, stirring, until the mushrooms are tender, about 7 minutes. Stir in the stewed tomatoes, tomato puree, water, oregano, basil, pepper, and salt. Reduce the heat to low and simmer for 20 minutes, stirring occasionally. Stir in the basil and remove from the heat.

Meanwhile, in a large saucepan, bring 3 quarts of water to a boil. Place the penne in the boiling water, stir, and return to a boil. Cook until al dente, stirring occasionally, 9 to 11 minutes. Drain in a colander and transfer to warm serving plates.

Spoon the sauce over the pasta. Serve with warm Italian bread.

Makes 4 servings

Helpful Hints

You can find fresh cremini, oyster, and shiitake mushrooms in the produce section of well-stocked grocery stores.

Parmesan cheese makes a natural garnish.

Per Serving:
447 Calories; 15g Protein; 9g Fat; 81g Carbohydrates; 0 Cholesterol; 695mg Sodium; 8g Fiber.

Spinach Pasta with Beet-Broccoli Marinara Sauce

Beets and broccoli add a healthful chunkiness to this classic marinara sauce. The green hue of spinach pasta nicely balances the sauce's magenta color.

1 tablespoon olive oil
1 medium yellow onion, diced
2 cloves garlic, minced
One 28-ounce can plum tomatoes
1 teaspoon dried oregano
1 teaspoon dried basil
½ teaspoon freshly ground black pepper
½ teaspoon salt
12 ounces spinach linguine
One 15-ounce can medium-size beets, diced
8 to 10 broccoli florets
¼ cup chopped fresh parsley

In a large saucepan, heat the oil over medium heat. Add the onion and garlic and cook, stirring, until the onion is translucent, about 4 minutes. Add the tomatoes, oregano, basil, pepper, and salt, and bring to a simmer. Cook for 15 to 20 minutes over medium-low heat, stirring occasionally.

Meanwhile, in a large saucepan, bring 3 quarts of water to a boil over medium-high heat. Place the linguine in the boiling water, stir, and return to a boil. Cook until al dente, stirring occasionally, 8 to 10 minutes. Drain in a colander and set aside until the tomato sauce is done.

Transfer the tomato sauce to a blender or a food processor fitted with a steel blade and process until smooth, about 5 seconds. Return the sauce to the pan and stir in the beets, broccoli, and parsley. Return to a gentle simmer over medium heat. Cook until the broccoli is tender, 3 to 5 minutes.

Place the linguine in a shallow serving dish. Ladle the sauce over the top and serve immediately.

Makes 4 servings

Per Serving:
369 Calories; 12g Protein; 5g Fat; 69g Carbohydrates; 0 Cholesterol; 1,017mg Sodium; 9g Fiber.

Helpful Hint

A smoky cheese, such as Gouda or provolone, makes an appealing topping.

Cavatelli with Spinach-Arugula Ricotta Sauce

This light green ricotta sauce clings nicely to chewy cavatelli pasta. Arugula lends an herbal presence to the dish.

1 pound frozen cavatelli
2 teaspoons canola oil
1 small yellow onion, diced
2 cloves garlic, minced
One 10-ounce package fresh
    spinach, rinsed, stems
    removed, and coarsely
    chopped
½ cup arugula leaves, coarsely
    chopped
1 teaspoon salt
½ teaspoon freshly ground
    black pepper
1 cup part-skim ricotta cheese
¼ chopped pimiento (optional)

In a large saucepan, bring 3 quarts of water to a boil over medium-high heat. Place the cavatelli in the boiling water, stir, and return to a medium boil (not rolling). Cook until al dente, stirring occasionally, 4 to 5 minutes. Drain in a colander and transfer to a warm, large serving dish.

In another large saucepan or wok, heat the oil over medium heat. Add the onion and garlic and cook, stirring, for 3 to 4 minutes. Add the spinach, arugula, salt, and pepper, and cook, stirring, until the greens are wilted, about 4 minutes.

Transfer the spinach mixture and the ricotta cheese to a blender or a food processor fitted with a steel blade. Process until smooth, 5 to 10 seconds.

In the large serving dish, combine the ricotta sauce, pimiento, if desired, and cooked cavatelli and toss together. Serve immediately.

Makes 4 servings

Per Serving:
445 Calories; 20g Protein; 9g Fat; 73g Carbohydrates; 19mg Cholesterol; 718mg Sodium; 7g Fiber.

Pasta e Fagioli

This classic Italian soup combines tiny pasta with hearty beans and garden vegetables (fagioli means "beans" in Italian). Acini de peppe, also called tubettini, and conchigliette piccole are two popular choices for the soup.

1 tablespoon olive oil
1 medium yellow onion, diced
1 small zucchini, diced
10 to 12 mushrooms, sliced
4 cloves garlic, minced
6 cups vegetable broth or
    water
1 large potato, diced (peeled if
    desired)
2 teaspoons dried oregano
1½ teaspoons dried basil
1 teaspoon salt
½ teaspoon freshly ground
    black pepper
½ cup acini di peppe (tubettini)
    or conchigliette piccole
½ cup tomato paste
One 15-ounce can cannelini
    beans
¼ cup chopped basil or parsley
Freshly grated Parmesan
    cheese to taste (optional)

In a large saucepan, heat the oil. Add the onion, zucchini, mushrooms, and garlic and cook for 7 minutes over medium heat, stirring frequently. Add the broth or water, potato, oregano, basil, salt, and pepper, and bring to a simmer. Cook for 10 to 12 minutes over medium-high heat, stirring occasionally.

Stir in the pasta, tomato paste, and beans, and cook over medium heat until the pasta is al dente, 12 to 15 minutes more. Occasionally stir the soup while it cooks.

Stir in the basil or parsley, and let the soup stand for 5 to 10 minutes before serving. Garnish with Parmesan if desired. Serve with warm Italian bread.

Makes 6 servings

Per Serving:
221 Calories; 11g Protein; 4g Fat;
42g Carbohydrates; 0 Cholesterol;
1,650mg Sodium; 6g Fiber.

Tomato Tortellini and Green Bean Soup

This soothing tureen of vegetables, tomato broth, and tortellini can be served as a satisfying soup or nourishing one-pot meal.

1 tablespoon canola oil
1 medium yellow onion, diced
10 to 12 mushrooms, sliced
4 cloves garlic, minced
6 cups vegetable broth
2 carrots, diced
2 teaspoons dried oregano
1 teaspoon dried basil
½ teaspoon salt
½ teaspoon freshly ground
　black pepper
4 ounces dried spinach or
　cheese tortellini (about
　1 cup)
⅓ pound green beans, trimmed
　and cut into 1-inch pieces
One 14-ounce can crushed
　tomatoes

In a large saucepan, heat the oil over medium heat. Add the onion, mushrooms, and garlic and cook, stirring, for 7 minutes.

Add the broth, carrots, oregano, basil, salt, and pepper, and bring to a simmer over high heat. Stir in the tortellini and green beans, and cook for 10 minutes over medium heat, stirring occasionally.

Stir in the crushed tomatoes, and cook until the tortellini is al dente, 7 to 10 minutes, stirring occasionally.

Let the soup sit for 5 to 10 minutes before serving. Serve with warm Italian bread.

Makes 6 servings

Per Serving:
119 Calories; 5g Protein; 5g Fat; 17g Carbohydrates; 4mg Cholesterol; 1,218mg Sodium; 3g Fiber.

Ravioli Stew

Serve this quick and colorful stew with crusty Italian bread.

One 14½-ounce can vegetable
    broth
½ cup water
1 teaspoon bottled minced,
    roasted garlic or minced
    fresh garlic
¼ to ½ teaspoon crushed red
    pepper flakes, as desired
One 9-ounce package fresh,
    light cheese ravioli
One 14½-ounce can Italian-style
    stewed tomatoes or diced
    tomatoes, undrained
2 cups packed, torn escarole or
    curly endive
1 tablespoon rosemary- or basil-
    infused olive oil (optional;
    see Helpful Hint)

Combine the broth, water, garlic, and pepper flakes in a large saucepan; bring to a boil over high heat.

Add the ravioli; simmer, uncovered, 3 minutes. Add the tomatoes; return to a simmer. Stir in the escarole or endive; simmer until the ravioli is cooked through and escarole is wilted, 2 to 3 minutes. Ladle into shallow bowls. Drizzle with olive oil, if desired.

Makes 4 servings

Helpful Hint

Flavored oils are available in gourmet food shops and in many supermarkets.

Per Serving:
119 Calories; 6g Protein; 2g Fat;
20g Carbohydrates; 4mg Cholesterol; 802mg Sodium; 3g Fiber.

New Mexico Corn and Pasta Chowder

This sweet-spicy chowder is sure to please the hearty soup lovers in your family. Look for tomatillo or green chili salsa in the ethnic section of your supermarket.

1½ cups (5 ounces) small tricol-
    ored soup shells
One 14½-ounce can creamed
    corn
1½ cups 2 percent milk or soy
    milk
1 cup prepared salsa or toma-
    tillo salsa
1 teaspoon ground cumin
3 scallions, sliced (about ¾ cup)
3 tablespoons chopped cilantro
1 cup (4 ounces) shredded
    sharp cheddar cheese
    (optional)

In a large saucepan, bring 3 quarts of water to a boil. Place the soup shells in the boiling water, stir, and return to a boil. Cook until al dente, stirring occasionally, 8 to 10 minutes.

Meanwhile, combine the corn, milk, salsa, and cumin in a medium saucepan. Bring to a simmer; simmer over low heat 5 minutes.

Drain the pasta in a colander. Add pasta and scallions to saucepan; simmer 5 minutes. Ladle into bowls; top with cilantro. Sprinkle with cheese, if desired.

Makes 4 servings

Per Serving:
211 Calories; 13g Protein; 3g Fat; 39g Carbohydrates; 7mg Cholesterol; 534mg Sodium; 3g Fiber.

Egg-Lemon Soup

Eggs act as a thickener for this traditional Greek soup and are cooked as they are stirred slowly into the soup just before serving.

Two 14½-ounce cans vegetable broth
1 cup water
¼ teaspoon ground white pepper
¾ cup (5 ounces) orzo
2 large eggs
2 tablespoons fresh lemon juice
2 tablespoons chopped fresh dill or parsley (optional)

Combine the broth, water, and pepper in a large saucepan; cover and bring to a boil over high heat. Stir in the orzo; simmer, uncovered, until orzo is tender, 12 to 14 minutes.

Just before the orzo is done, beat together the eggs and lemon juice in a small bowl. After orzo is cooked, turn off the heat, and pour the egg mixture very slowly in a stream into the soup while stirring constantly. Ladle into bowls; top with dill or parsley, if desired.

Makes 4 servings

Per Serving:
134 Calories; 7g Protein; 4g Fat; 20g Carbohydrates; 106mg Cholesterol; 470mg Sodium; 1g Fiber.

Creole Vegetables and Pasta

Traditional Creole sauces cook for hours and tend to be oily, but this version is quick and, of course, keeps oil to a minimum. Creole or blackened seasonings will give the dish a spicy note, but serve with hot sauce at the table so that everyone can achieve the level of "heat" they desire.

8 ounces tricolored quinoa pagodas or regular radiatore (see Helpful Hints)
2 tablespoons vegetable or olive oil
1½ cups chopped onion
3 medium carrots, thinly sliced
2 stalks celery, sliced
1 green bell pepper, diced
2 teaspoons minced garlic
1 tablespoon Creole seasonings or blackened seasonings
1 tablespoon all-purpose flour
One 14½-ounce can Cajun-style or regular stewed tomatoes, undrained
2 cups water
2 teaspoons dried thyme leaves
1 teaspoon gumbo filé powder (see Helpful Hint)
¼ cup chopped flat-leaf parsley
Hot pepper sauce to taste

Cook pasta according to package directions.

Meanwhile, heat oil in a large saucepan over medium heat. Add the onion, carrots, celery, and bell pepper to the saucepan. Reduce heat to low, cover tightly, and sweat (lightly steam) the vegetables 8 minutes.

Add the garlic and Creole or blackened seasonings; cook, stirring, 1 minute. Sprinkle the flour over the vegetables; cook 1 minute, stirring frequently.

Add the tomatoes, water, and thyme; bring to a boil. Simmer, uncovered, until the vegetables are crisp-tender, about 5 minutes, stirring occasionally. Remove from heat; stir in the filé powder.

Drain the pasta in a colander; transfer to shallow bowls. Top with the Creole sauce; sprinkle with parsley. Serve with hot pepper sauce.

Makes 6 servings

Per Serving:
237 Calories; 6g Protein; 6g Fat; 41g Carbohydrates; 0 Cholesterol; 172mg Sodium; 5g Fiber.

Helpful Hints

Quinoa is a high-protein grain from South America that formed the basis of the diet of the ancient Incas. Its grains look like tiny beads and cook up much like rice. Flour from the grain is used for various foods. Quinoa pagoda pasta looks like small radiatore; the tricolored variety also contains corn flour, red bell peppers, and spinach. Quinoa products are available in natural food stores and in many supermarkets.

Filé powder, also called gumbo filé, is a seasoning made from the ground, dried leaves of the sassafras tree. It's an integral seasoning in Creole cuisine.

Bistro Penne Rigate

8 ounces penne rigate, penne, or mostaccioli

2 cups cut fresh asparagus spears (1-inch diagonal pieces)

1 recipe (3½ cups) Herbed Artichoke-Tomato Sauce (page 176)

4 ounces goat cheese or herbed goat cheese, crumbled (optional)

¼ cup packed, thinly sliced basil leaves

Freshly ground black pepper

In a large saucepan, bring 3 quarts of water to a boil. Place the pasta in the boiling water, stir, and return to a boil. Cook until al dente, stirring occasionally, 8 to 10 minutes, adding asparagus to pasta cooking water during last 4 minutes of cooking.

Meanwhile, prepare Herbed Artichoke-Tomato Sauce.

Drain pasta and asparagus in a colander and return to the pot. Add sauce; toss well. Spoon onto serving plates. Top with cheese, if desired. Sprinkle with basil and serve with pepper.

Makes 4 servings

Per Serving:
358 Calories; 13g Protein; 5g Fat;
66g Carbohydrates; 0 Cholesterol;
519mg Sodium; 6g Fiber.

Spaghetti Santa Fe

*Serve this sassy dish with melon wedges and warm corn tortillas
for a true taste of the Southwest.*

**8 ounces whole wheat or
 regular spaghetti**
**2 tablespoons vegetable or
 olive oil**
1½ cups chopped onion
**1 red or green bell pepper,
 diced**
3 cloves garlic, minced
**One 14½-ounce can salsa-style
 or chili-style diced or
 stewed tomatoes,
 undrained**
**½ cup prepared salsa or picante
 sauce**
1 teaspoon ground cumin
**One 15-ounce can black beans,
 rinsed and drained**
1 cup frozen corn kernels
¼ cup chopped cilantro
**1 cup (4 ounces) crumbled
 queso fresco or queso anejo
 cheese (optional; see Helpful Hint)**

In a large saucepan, bring 3 quarts
of water to a boil. Place the spaghetti in the boiling water, stir,
and return to a boil. Cook until al
dente, stirring occasionally,
8 to 10 minutes.

Meanwhile, heat oil in a large
deep skillet over medium heat.
Add onion and bell pepper; cover
and cook 5 minutes. Add garlic
and cook, stirring, 2 minutes.

Stir in tomatoes, salsa or
picante, and cumin; simmer 5
minutes. Stir in beans and corn;
simmer, uncovered, 5 minutes,
stirring occasionally.

Drain pasta in a colander and
add to the skillet. Toss to coat
pasta with sauce; transfer to four
serving plates and top with
cilantro. Sprinkle with cheese, if
desired.

Makes 4 servings

Helpful Hint

*Queso fresco and queso anejo are
Mexican cheeses similar to farmer
cheese. They are sold in tubs or as
shrink-wrapped rounds in Mexican
groceries and many supermarkets.*

Per Serving:
433 Calories; 19g Protein; 9g Fat;
77g Carbohydrates; 0 Cholesterol;
592mg Sodium; 16g Fiber.

Quick Macaroni and Cheese

Look no further for a creamy, cheesy macaroni and cheese that is not only quick to prepare but wholesome as well.

One 7-ounce package elbow macaroni or conchigliette piccole, or one 8-ounce package quinoa pasta
1 tablespoon butter
2 cloves garlic, minced
⅛ teaspoon cayenne pepper
1 tablespoon all-purpose flour
1 cup canned evaporated skim milk
¼ teaspoon salt
1¼ cups (5 ounces) low-fat shredded Cheddar cheese

In a large saucepan, bring 3 quarts of water to a boil. Place the pasta in the boiling water, stir, and return to a boil. Cook until al dente, stirring occasionally, 8 to 10 minutes. (If using quinoa pasta, prepare according to package directions.)

Meanwhile, melt the butter in a medium saucepan. Add the garlic and cayenne pepper; cook 1 minute over medium heat. Add the flour; cook 1 minute, stirring constantly. Add the evaporated milk and salt; bring to a simmer, stirring frequently. Simmer 2 minutes. Reduce heat to low; stir in 1 cup of the cheese.

Drain the pasta in a colander; add it to saucepan with the cheese sauce. Cook 1 minute. Transfer to serving plates; sprinkle with remaining ¼ cup cheese.

Makes 6 servings

Per Serving:
238 Calories; 14g Protein; 6g Fat; 31g Carbohydrates; 153mg Cholesterol; 336mg Sodium; 1g Fiber.

Ziti with Sun-Dried Tomatoes and Asparagus

*The addition of sun-dried tomatoes and asparagus makes this fancy enough
for company, easy enough for every day.*

8 ounces ziti or a medium-shape, wheat-free pasta such as quinoa
One 14½-ounce can vegetable broth
¼ teaspoon crushed red pepper flakes
One 2-ounce package sun-dried tomatoes (about ½ cup; not oil-packed variety)
3 cups diagonally sliced, 1-inch pieces fresh asparagus
¼ teaspoon salt, or to taste
2 tablespoons garlic- or rosemary-infused olive oil or extra-virgin olive oil
1 cup (4 ounces) freshly grated Asiago or Parmesan cheese (optional)

In a large saucepan, bring 3 quarts of water to a boil. Place the pasta in the boiling water, stir, and return to a boil. Cook until al dente, stirring occasionally, 8 to 10 minutes. (If using a wheat-free pasta, prepare according to package directions.)

Meanwhile, bring the broth and the pepper flakes to a boil in a medium saucepan. Cut the tomatoes with scissors or a sharp knife into ¼-inch pieces; add to the saucepan with the broth mixture. Simmer, uncovered, 5 minutes, stirring occasionally.

Add the asparagus and salt to saucepan; simmer until the asparagus is crisp-tender, about 2 to 3 minutes.

Drain the pasta in a colander and return it to the pot. Add the broth mixture; toss well. Transfer to serving plates; drizzle with the oil. Serve with cheese if desired.

Makes 4 servings

Per Serving:
323 Calories; 10g Protein; 8g Fat;
54g Carbohydrates; 0 Cholesterol;
583mg Sodium; 3g Fiber.

Orecchiette, Broccoli, and Mushroom Ragout

8 ounces orecchiette
2 cups broccoli florets
½ ounce dried morel, oyster, or
    mixed mushrooms
1 cup boiling water
2 tablespoons olive oil or butter
1¼ cups chopped onion (about
    2 medium onions)
8 ounces fresh oyster, cremini,
    morel, or chanterelle
    mushrooms, or a mixture,
    halved if large
4 cloves garlic, minced
¼ cup dry red wine such as
    Cabernet Sauvignon
2 teaspoons dried herbes de
    Provence, fines herbes, or
    1 teaspoon dried basil plus
    1 teaspoon dried thyme (see
    Helpful Hints)
½ teaspoon salt, or to taste
Freshly ground black pepper

In a large saucepan, bring 3 quarts of water to a boil. Place the pasta in the boiling water, stir, and return to a boil. Cook until al dente, stirring occasionally, 8 to 10 minutes, adding the broccoli to the cooking water during the last 2 to 3 minutes of cooking time.

Meanwhile, cut the dried mushrooms into ½-inch pieces with scissors or a sharp knife. Place them in a small bowl and pour the boiling water over them; let stand 10 minutes.

Heat the oil or butter in a large, deep skillet over medium heat. Add the onion and cook, stirring, for 5 minutes. Add the fresh mushrooms and garlic and cook, stirring, for 3 minutes. Add the wine, herbs, and salt and cook 1 minute. Add the dried mushrooms with the soaking water and cook 5 minutes more.

Drain the pasta and broccoli in a colander and add to the skillet with the mushroom mixture. Simmer until heated through, 1 to 2 minutes. Ladle into shallow bowls; sprinkle with pepper to taste.

Makes 6 servings

Per Serving:
232 Calories; 8g Protein; 6g Fat;
37g Carbohydrates; 0 Cholesterol;
209mg Sodium; 3g Fiber.

Helpful Hints

Herbes de Provence is a blend of dried herbs that commonly flavors the cuisine of Provence, France. The blend usually consists of dried basil, rosemary, sage, thyme, lavender, summer savory, and fennel seed. Look for packaged herbes de Provence in the spice aisle of your supermarket or in gourmet food shops.

Fines herbes is a mixture of chopped fresh chives, parsley, tarragon, and chervil.

Exotic Mushroom Linguine

8 ounces dried or 10 ounces fresh mushroom- or tomato-flavored linguine or fettuccine

One 14½-ounce can vegetable broth

½ ounce dried porcini mushrooms

2 tablespoons olive oil

½ cup sliced shallots or chopped sweet onion

8 ounces fresh sliced exotic mushrooms (such as oyster, cremini, and shiitake) or button mushrooms, sliced

3 cloves garlic, minced

1 tablespoon chopped fresh thyme or 1 teaspoon dried, plus more fresh thyme or thyme sprigs for optional garnish

¼ to ½ teaspoon freshly ground black pepper

¼ teaspoon salt, or to taste

2 teaspoons cornstarch

1 tablespoon cold water

In a large saucepan, bring 3 quarts of water to a boil. Place the linguine or fettuccine in the boiling water, stir, and return to a boil. Cook until al dente, stirring occasionally, about 8 to 10 minutes. If using fresh pasta, cook 4 to 5 minutes.

Meanwhile, bring the broth to a simmer in a small saucepan. Using scissors or a sharp knife, cut the dried porcini mushrooms into ¼-inch pieces; add to the saucepan with the broth. Simmer, uncovered, 10 minutes.

Meanwhile, heat the oil in a large, deep skillet over medium heat until hot. Add the shallots or onion, and cook 3 minutes. Add the fresh mushrooms, garlic, thyme, pepper, and salt and cook 3 minutes. Pour the broth mixture into the skillet with the mushroom mixture and simmer, uncovered, 3 minutes.

In a cup or small bowl, stir cornstarch and cold water to form a smooth paste; stir into the skillet. Simmer until thickened, 1 to 2 minutes.

Drain linguine; transfer to serving plates. Spoon mushroom mixture over linguine, and garnish with extra thyme or thyme sprigs, if desired.

Makes 4 servings

Per Serving:
261 Calories; 8g Protein; 8g Fat; 41g Carbohydrates; 0 Cholesterol; 564mg Sodium; 3g Fiber.

Capellini, Pepper, and Pesto Toss

Using packaged, frozen bell pepper and onion strips saves time otherwise spent chopping. And if you keep Pesto-Style Sauce (page 178) on hand in the freezer, you can have this meal in minutes.

One 16-ounce package frozen bell pepper and onion strips
8 ounces capellini, broken in half
2 cups (1 recipe) Pesto-Style Sauce (see Helpful Hint)
4 ounces diced fat-free soy mozzarella cheese or fresh mozzarella cheese
Salt and freshly ground black pepper to taste

Bring a large pot of water to a boil over medium-high heat. Add the bell pepper and onion strips. Return to a boil, and stir in the capellini. After the water returns to a boil again, cook until the capellini is al dente and the vegetables are hot, about 2 minutes. Drain in a colander, and return capellini and vegetables to the pot.

Add the pesto sauce; toss to coat. Cook over medium heat until pasta and peppers are coated with sauce, about 1 minute. Add the cheese, and toss again. Season to taste with salt and pepper if desired.

Makes 4 servings

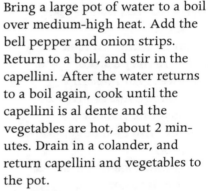

Helpful Hint

Make the pesto sauce while the water comes to a boil. To thaw Pesto-Style Sauce if you have previously made it, cook at 50 percent power (medium) for 7 minutes in a microwave oven. Stir and continue cooking until thawed, 7 to 8 minutes more.

Per Serving:
366 Calories; 21g Protein; 11g Fat; 47g Carbohydrates; 70mg Cholesterol; 883mg Sodium; 5g Fiber.

Vegetable Goulash with Egg Noodles

1 tablespoon olive or vegetable oil

1¼ cups chopped onion (about 2 medium onions)

1 green or red bell pepper, diced

4 cloves garlic, minced

2 teaspoons paprika, preferably sweet Hungarian

¼ teaspoon hot paprika or cayenne pepper

One 14½-ounce can vegetable broth

One 14½-ounce can stewed tomatoes or Cajun-style stewed tomatoes, undrained

1 cup frozen corn kernels

1 teaspoon dried oregano, marjoram, or basil

1½ cups (3 ounces) thin egg noodles

Sour cream (optional)

Heat the oil in a large saucepan over medium-high heat. Add the onion, bell pepper, and garlic, and cook, stirring, for 5 minutes. Sprinkle sweet and hot paprikas or cayenne over the bell pepper mixture and cook another 30 seconds.

Add the broth, tomatoes, corn, oregano, marjoram, or basil; cover and bring to a boil over high heat. Stir in the noodles; return to a boil. Reduce heat; cover and simmer until the noodles are tender, about 7 minutes. Ladle into shallow bowls. Garnish with sour cream if desired.

Makes 4 servings

Per Serving:
364 Calories; 12g Protein; 7g Fat; 67g Carbohydrates; 53mg Cholesterol; 772mg Sodium; 6g Fiber.

Caponata-Style Pasta Supper

**7 to 8 ounces brown rice rotini
    or whole wheat rotini**
**1 tablespoon olive oil or garlic-
    or basil-infused olive oil**
**3 cups peeled, diced eggplant
    (1 small eggplant)**
**1 large or 2 small zucchini
    squash, cut into ½-inch
    chunks (about 2 cups)**
2 cloves garlic, minced
**2 cups (½ recipe) Puttanesca
    Sauce (page 173)**
**Freshly grated Asiago or
    Parmesan cheese (optional)**

In a large saucepan, bring 3 quarts of water to a boil. Place the pasta in the boiling water, stir, and return to a boil. Cook until al dente, stirring occasionally, 8 to 10 minutes.

Meanwhile, heat the oil in a large nonstick skillet over medium heat. Add the eggplant, zucchini, and garlic and cook, stirring, for 10 minutes.

Add the Puttanesca Sauce and simmer, covered, until the vegetables are tender, about 5 minutes. Drain the rotini in a colander and add it to the skillet with the eggplant mixture. Toss to coat the rotini with the sauce, and transfer to shallow bowls. Sprinkle with cheese if desired.

Makes 4 servings

Per Serving:
302 Calories; 8g Protein; 8g Fat;
53g Carbohydrates; 0 Cholesterol;
120mg Sodium; 6g Fiber.

Minestrone Soup

Traditional minestrone in thirty minutes? No problem, especially if you use packaged chopped vegetables from the freezer case or the supermarket produce section.

1 tablespoon olive oil
1 cup chopped onion
¾ cup coarsely grated carrots
1 teaspoon minced garlic
Two 14½-ounce cans vegetable broth
¾ cup ditalini, soup shell, or tricolored soup shell pasta (2 ounces)
½ cup water
One 14½-ounce can Italian-style, diced tomatoes, undrained
1 cup rinsed and drained canned cannellini, great Northern, or red kidney beans
1 teaspoon dried basil
½ teaspoon dried oregano or marjoram
¼ teaspoon red pepper flakes
¾ cup frozen peas
¼ cup chopped fresh basil or flat-leaf parsley (optional)
¼ cup freshly grated Parmesan cheese (optional)

Heat the oil in large saucepan over medium-high heat. Add the onion, carrots, and garlic and cook, stirring, for 4 minutes.

Add the broth, pasta, and water; cover and bring to a boil over high heat. Reduce heat to low and simmer 10 minutes.

Stir in the tomatoes, beans, basil, oregano or marjoram, and pepper flakes; return to a simmer. Simmer, uncovered, 5 minutes.

Stir in the peas; simmer until peas are hot and pasta is tender, about 2 minutes. Stir in the fresh basil or parsley, if desired. Ladle into shallow bowls and top with the cheese, if desired.

Makes 5 servings

Per Serving:
196 Calories; 10g Protein; 5g Fat; 31g Carbohydrates; 0 Cholesterol; 1,075mg Sodium; 7g Fiber.

Mediterranean Orzo "Risotto"

Not a risotto in the traditional sense, but still a delicious, fast, and easy alternative.

8 ounces orzo
2 tablespoons olive oil
½ cup chopped shallots or
    onion
2 cups diced bell peppers,
    preferably red and yellow
    (about 2 peppers)
4 cloves garlic, minced
1 medium zucchini squash,
    diced
1 medium yellow squash, diced
2 tablespoons chopped fresh
    thyme or 2 teaspoons dried
½ teaspoon salt, or to taste
¼ teaspoon freshly ground
    black pepper
One 6-ounce can spicy or
    regular vegetable juice
    (¾ cup)
Shaved Parmesan or Asiago
    cheese (optional)

In a large saucepan, bring 2 quarts of water to a boil. Place the orzo in the boiling water, stir, and return to a boil. Cook until almost al dente, stirring occasionally, about 1 minute less than package directions.

Meanwhile, heat the oil in a large, deep skillet over medium heat. Add the shallots or onion and cook, stirring, 4 minutes.

Add the bell peppers and garlic and cook, stirring, 4 minutes. Add the zucchini and yellow squash and cook, stirring, 4 minutes more. Sprinkle thyme, salt, and pepper over vegetables.

Drain the orzo and add it to the skillet with the vegetable mixture. Stir in the vegetable juice and simmer over low heat until it thickens, about 2 minutes. Top with cheese, if desired.

Makes 4 servings

Per Serving:
212 Calories; 6g Protein; 8g Fat; 32g Carbohydrates; 0 Cholesterol; 466mg Sodium; 4g Fiber.

Hot and Sour Noodle Soup

An Asian favorite.

Two 14½-ounce cans vegetable broth
1 cup plus 2 tablespoons water
3 ounces thin soba (buckwheat) or somen noodles
One 15-ounce can straw mushrooms, drained (see Helpful Hints)
½ cup finely diced red bell pepper
½ cup drained canned bamboo shoots, cut in half lengthwise
3 tablespoons rice vinegar or white vinegar
2 tablespoons tamari (see Helpful Hints) or soy sauce
1½ teaspoons hot chili oil (see Helpful Hints)
About 5 ounces (½ of a 10½-ounce package) low-fat, extra-firm tofu, diced
2 teaspoons cornstarch
2 egg whites, slightly beaten (optional)
½ cup thinly sliced scallions
2 teaspoons sesame oil

Combine the broth, 1 cup of the water, and noodles in a large saucepan. Bring to a boil over high heat. Reduce heat to medium-low and simmer 2 minutes. Stir in the mushrooms, bell pepper, and bamboo shoots. Simmer, uncovered, 4 minutes.

Add the vinegar, tamari or soy sauce, and chili oil to the noodle mixture, and simmer 1 minute. Stir in the tofu; simmer 1 minute more.

In a cup or a small bowl, combine the remaining 2 tablespoons water and cornstarch, stirring until smooth. Stir the cornstarch paste into the soup and simmer 1 minute, stirring once. If desired, slowly pour in the beaten egg whites while stirring the soup in one direction. Stir in scallions and sesame oil; ladle into soup bowls.

Makes 4 servings

VARIATION

Substitute a 3-ounce package of ramen noodles for the soba or somen. (Use the enclosed flavor packet for another purpose.)

Per Serving:
199 Calories; 10g Protein; 6g Fat; 30g Carbohydrates; 0 Cholesterol; 1,376mg Sodium; 2g Fiber.

Helpful Hints

Straw mushrooms are small, tannish-gray mushrooms so-named because they are grown on straw. They are sometimes available dried in gourmet food shops, but are widely available canned in supermarkets.

Tamari is a naturally brewed, strong-flavored soy sauce that contains no sugar and usually no wheat. It is available in supermarkets, natural food stores, and Asian groceries.

Hot chili oil is vegetable oil infused with hot chili peppers. It is sold in supermarkets and natural food stores.

Tomato-Basil Frittata

This hearty omelet makes a meal when served with crusty bread and tossed salad greens.

Nonstick cooking spray
½ cup sliced scallions
2 cloves garlic, minced
5 large egg whites
1 large egg yolk
¼ cup canned, evaporated skim milk or soy milk
½ teaspoon salt
¼ teaspoon freshly ground black pepper or red pepper flakes
1 cup cooked whole wheat or regular spaghetti
½ cup diced, seeded plum tomatoes
¼ cup thinly sliced, fresh basil leaves
¼ cup (1 ounce) grated Asiago cheese (optional)

Preheat oven to 450°F.

Coat a 10-inch, ovenproof, nonstick skillet with sloped sides with cooking spray. Add the scallions and garlic to the skillet, and cook, stirring, over medium heat 3 minutes.

In a medium bowl, beat together the egg whites, egg yolk, milk, salt, and pepper or pepper flakes. Stir in the spaghetti, tomatoes, and basil.

Pour spaghetti mixture into the skillet over the scallion mixture. Mix well, and spread the ingredients evenly in skillet. Reduce the heat to medium-low, and cook until almost set, about 5 minutes. Sprinkle with cheese, if desired.

Place skillet in oven and bake until set, about 5 minutes more.

Makes 4 servings

Per Serving:
106 Calories; 10g Protein; 2g Fat; 14g Carbohydrates; 54mg Cholesterol; 450mg Sodium; 2g Fiber.

Red Lentil and Orzo Soup

Red lentils, paired with orzo, make a colorful and flavorful Italian-style soup, and cook up quickly.

Two 14-½ ounce cans vegetable broth
3 cups water
½ cup orzo
½ cup red lentils
One 16-ounce package frozen mixed vegetables, such as peas, carrots, lima beans, and corn, etc.
½ teaspoon salt, or to taste
¼ teaspoon freshly ground black pepper
2 tablespoons chopped assorted mixed herbs, such as thyme, basil, oregano
2 tablespoons chopped fresh chives or flat-leaf parsley
2 tablespoons garlic-infused olive oil (optional)

Combine the broth, water, orzo, and lentils in a large saucepan. Cover and bring to a boil over high heat. Reduce heat to medium-low and simmer, uncovered, for 15 minutes.

Stir in frozen vegetables, salt, and pepper, cover and return to a boil over high heat. Reduce heat to medium-low; simmer until orzo, lentils and vegetables are tender, about 5 minutes more.

Stir in herbs, chives or parsley, and, if desired, oil; simmer 1 minute. Ladle into soup bowls; sprinkle with additional pepper, if desired.

Makes 6 servings

Per Serving:
162 Calories; 10g Protein; 1g Fat;
32g Carbohydrates; 0 Cholesterol;
826mg Sodium; 10g Fiber.

Paella Pasta Ragout

8 ounces whole wheat or tricolored medium conchiglie

1 small fennel bulb (about 8 ounces)

1 tablespoon olive oil

1 yellow bell pepper, coarsely chopped (1½ cups)

4 cloves garlic, minced

One 14½-ounce can vegetable broth

One 14½-ounce can Italian-style, diced tomatoes, undrained

½ to ¾ teaspoon hot pepper sauce, or to taste

½ teaspoon saffron threads (see Helpful Hint) or ground turmeric

1 tablespoon water

2 teaspoons cornstarch

¾ cup frozen peas

¼ teaspoon salt, or to taste

In a large saucepan, bring 3 quarts of water to a boil. Place the pasta in the boiling water, stir, and return to a boil. Cook, stirring occasionally, until al dente, 8 to 10 minutes.

Meanwhile, chop the fennel bulb, reserving the feathery fronds for garnish.

Heat the oil in a large, deep skillet over medium-high heat. Add the fennel bulb, bell pepper, and garlic, cover the skillet and sweat the vegetables 5 minutes.

Stir in the broth, tomatoes, hot pepper sauce, and saffron or turmeric; bring to a boil over high heat. Reduce heat; simmer, uncovered, 10 minutes, stirring occasionally. Combine water and cornstarch in a cup, mixing until smooth. Stir it into the broth mixture and simmer until sauce thickens, stirring occasionally, about 1 minute.

Stir in the peas and salt and simmer 1 minute. Drain the pasta in a colander, and add it to the skillet. Simmer 1 minute, tossing occasionally.

Ladle into shallow bowls; sprinkle with the reserved chopped fennel fronds, if desired.

Makes 5 servings

Helpful Hint

Always combine saffron threads with a little water or hot liquid from the dish you're cooking, and crush the threads with a wooden spoon or pestle before adding to the dish.

Per Serving:
264 Calories; 10g Protein; 4g Fat; 50g Carbohydrates; 0 Cholesterol; 669mg Sodium; 3g Fiber.

Rigatoni Primavera

8 ounces rigatoni or
   mostaccioli
8 ounces fresh baby carrots
2 tablespoons butter
1 small red or sweet onion,
   chopped
2 tablespoons all-purpose flour
One 14½-ounce can vegetable
   broth
1½ cups diagonally sliced
   asparagus spears (1-inch
   pieces) or baby pattypan
   squash
1 yellow or red bell pepper,
   julienned
1½ cups fresh sugar snap peas
   or snow peas, halved if
   large
½ teaspoon salt, or to taste
¼ cup chopped basil or mixed
   fresh herbs, such as tarragon, thyme, parsley, and
   mint
½ cup (2 ounces) crumbled feta
   cheese (optional)

In a large saucepan, bring 3 quarts of water to a boil. Place the pasta in the boiling water, stir, and return to a boil. Cook, stirring occasionally, until al dente, 8 to 10 minutes, adding the carrots to the pasta water during the last 6 minutes of cooking.

Meanwhile, melt the butter in a large, deep skillet over medium heat. Add the onion and cook, stirring, 3 minutes. Sprinkle with the flour and cook, stirring, 1 minute more.

Add the broth, asparagus, and bell pepper and bring to a boil over medium-high heat, stirring frequently. Stir in the peas and salt; reduce the heat to medium-low, and simmer, uncovered, until vegetables are crisp-tender, about 5 minutes.

Stir in the basil or herbs, and simmer 2 minutes.

Drain the pasta and carrots in a colander, and add them to the skillet with the broth mixture. Simmer until the pasta is coated with sauce, about 2 minutes. Stir in the cheese if desired.

Makes 6 servings

Per Serving:
238 Calories; 8g Protein; 5g Fat; 42g Carbohydrates; 10mg Cholesterol; 564mg Sodium; 5g Fiber.

Grilled Vegetables with Fresh Fettuccine

Many supermarket delis now sell freshly made pasta. If it is not available in your market, substitute two nine-ounce packages of the prepared, refrigerated variety.

2 large or 3 medium portabella mushrooms (about 12 ounces)

1 medium zucchini, halved lengthwise

1 medium yellow squash or zucchini, halved lengthwise

1 red or yellow bell pepper, quartered

1 medium eggplant, cut lengthwise into four ½-inch slices

¼ cup fat-free or reduced-fat Italian or honey-mustard salad dressing

1 pound fresh flavored or plain fettuccine

2 tablespoons garlic-infused oil or extra-virgin olive oil

¼ teaspoon salt, or to taste

¼ teaspoon freshly ground black pepper

¼ cup chopped fresh basil or oregano

4 ounces goat cheese or herbed goat cheese (optional)

Preheat grill or broiler.

Brush all sides of the mushrooms and vegetables with the dressing. Place on a grill or nonstick broiler rack and grill or broil 5 inches from heat source until tender, 5 to 6 minutes per side.

Meanwhile, in a large saucepan, bring 3 quarts of water to a boil. Place the fettuccine in the boiling water, stir, and return to a boil. Cook, stirring occasionally, until al dente, 3 to 5 minutes. Drain in a colander, return to pot, and toss with oil, salt, and pepper; transfer to serving platter.

Cut the grilled vegetables into chunks, and arrange them over the fettuccine. Sprinkle with the basil, and top with goat cheese, if desired.

Makes 6 servings

Per Serving:
302 Calories; 11g Protein; 7g Fat; 50g Carbohydrates; 0 Cholesterol; 217mg Sodium; 5g Fiber.

Gorgonzola Ravioli with Oyster Mushroom Ragout

Oyster mushrooms, available in most supermarkets, are grayish-brown, fan-shaped mushrooms with a slight peppery taste. Generally, the smaller the mushroom, the better the taste, so look for mushrooms less than two inches in diameter for the best flavor.

One 9-ounce package refrigerated gorgonzola and walnut ravioli
1 teaspoon olive oil
2 cloves garlic, minced
8 ounces fresh oyster mushrooms (halved if large) or sliced domestic mushrooms
2 tablespoons dry sherry
1 cup vegetable broth
1½ teaspoons cornstarch
1 tablespoon chopped fresh tarragon or 1 teaspoon dried
¼ teaspoon salt, or to taste
¼ teaspoon freshly ground black pepper
1 cup diced fresh tomato

In a large saucepan, bring 3 quarts of water to a boil. Place the ravioli in the boiling water, stir, and return to a boil. Cook, stirring occasionally, until al dente, 3 to 5 minutes.

Meanwhile, heat the oil in a large nonstick skillet over medium heat. Add the garlic and cook, stirring, 1 minute. Add the mushrooms, and cook, stirring, 5 minutes more. Add the sherry and cook 1 minute.

In a cup or small bowl, combine broth and cornstarch and mix until smooth. Add the cornstarch mixture, tarragon, salt, and pepper to skillet; simmer until mixture thickens slightly, stirring occasionally, about 5 minutes. Add the tomato and heat through.

Drain the ravioli, and transfer to four shallow bowls. Spoon mushroom mixture over ravioli, and serve hot.

Makes 4 servings

Per Serving:
271 Calories; 11g Protein; 10g Fat; 35g Carbohydrates; 23mg Cholesterol; 666mg Sodium; 6g Fiber.

Tomato Capellini with Two-Squash Pesto Sauce

**2 cups (1 recipe) Pesto-Style
 Sauce (page 178)**
**8 ounces tomato capellini
 (angel-hair pasta)**
**Nonstick olive oil cooking
 spray**
**1 small red or sweet onion,
 chopped**
1 medium yellow squash
1 medium zucchini
Salt and pepper to taste
**¼ cup pine nuts, toasted
 (optional)**
**Freshly grated Parmesano-
 Reggiano cheese
 (optional)**

Prepare the Pesto-Style Sauce, or thaw sauce if it was previously made and frozen (see Helpful Hint; page 49).

In a large saucepan, bring 3 quarts of water to a boil. Place the pasta in the boiling water, stir, and return to a boil. Cook, stirring occasionally, until al dente, about 2 to 3 minutes.

Meanwhile, coat a large nonstick skillet with cooking spray. Cook the onion, stirring, over medium heat for 5 minutes.

Meanwhile, cut the squash and zucchini crosswise into ¹/₂-inch slices, and cut each slice into quarters. Add the vegetables to the skillet with the onion, and cook, stirring, 5 more minutes.

Add the pesto sauce, and simmer, uncovered, until the vegetables are crisp-tender, 2 to 3 minutes. Season to taste with salt and pepper, if desired.

Drain the pasta in a colander and transfer to serving plates. Spoon vegetables and sauce over the pasta, and top with pine nuts and cheese, if desired.

Makes 4 servings

Per Serving:
286 Calories; 10g Protein; 10g Fat; 42g Carbohydrates; 4mg Cholesterol; 842mg Sodium; 3g Fiber.

Cowboy Pasta and Beans

Wagon wheel pasta shapes and chili-flavored beans—what else could this dish be called but Cowboy Pasta and Beans?

8 ounces whole wheat or regular rotelle (wagon wheel pasta)
1 tablespoon vegetable or olive oil
1 cup chopped onion
1½ cups chopped bell pepper, any color
4 cloves garlic, minced
One 15½-ounce can spicy chili beans, undrained
½ cup picante sauce or vegetable broth
1 teaspoon chili powder
1 teaspoon ground cumin
1 cup (4 ounces) shredded sharp cheddar cheese (optional)

In a large saucepan, bring 3 quarts of water to a boil. Place the pasta in the boiling water, stir, and return to a boil. Cook, stirring occasionally, until al dente, 8 to 10 minutes.

Meanwhile, heat the oil in a large, deep skillet over medium heat. Add the onion and cook, stirring, 5 minutes. Add the bell pepper and garlic and cook, stirring, 5 minutes more.

Stir in the beans, picante sauce or broth, chili powder, and cumin. Cover, reduce the heat to low, and simmer for 5 minutes. Drain the pasta in a colander, and transfer to a serving bowl or platter. Add the sauce and toss. Sprinkle with cheese, if desired.

Makes 5 servings

Per Serving:
239 Calories; 11g Protein; 4g Fat;
45g Carbohydrates; 0 Cholesterol;
566mg Sodium; 7g Fiber.

Cheese Tortellini with Broccoli and Gremolata

Gremolata is a flat-leaf parsley garnish flavored with garlic and lemon that gives this quick dish a vibrant, fresh kick.

One 8-ounce package dried tricolored cheese tortellini
3 cups broccoli florets or halved baby yellow pattypan squash
½ cup chopped flat-leaf parsley
1½ teaspoons finely shredded lemon peel
2 cloves garlic, minced
¾ cup vegetable broth
¼ teaspoon red pepper flakes
1 tablespoon garlic- or basil-infused olive oil
Salt and freshly ground black pepper to taste

In a large saucepan, bring 3 quarts of water to a boil. Place the tortellini in the boiling water, stir, and return to a boil. Cook, stirring occasionally, until al dente, 6 to 8 minutes, adding the broccoli or squash during the last 3 minutes of cooking.

Meanwhile, prepare the gremolata by combining the parsley, lemon peel, and garlic in a small bowl; mix well and set aside.

Drain the tortellini and broccoli or squash in a colander. Add the broth and the pepper flakes to the pasta cooking pot, and bring to a boil. Add the drained tortellini and broccoli or squash, and toss well. Add the gremolata, and toss again. Transfer to serving plates; drizzle with oil; season to taste with salt; and serve with pepper.

Makes 4 servings

Per Serving:
231 Calories; 11g Protein; 8g Fat; 31g Carbohydrates; 30mg Cholesterol; 576mg Sodium; 4g Fiber.

Tuscan White Bean and Pasta Pesto Soup

*This soup is brimming with traditional Tuscan ingredients and flavors:
pasta, beans, tomatoes, and pesto.*

1½ cups (5 ounces) small to
    medium pasta, such as
    ditalini, orecchiette, or
    gnocchi
One 14½-ounce can vegetable
    broth
One 14½-ounce can Italian-style
    diced tomatoes, undrained
One 16- to 19-ounce can
    cannellini beans or great
    Northern beans, rinsed and
    drained
1 tablespoon balsamic vinegar
3 tablespoons prepared pesto
    sauce
Garlic-flavored croutons
    (optional)

In a large saucepan, bring 3 quarts of water to a boil. Place the pasta in the boiling water, stir, and return to a boil. Cook, stirring occasionally, until al dente, 8 to 10 minutes.

Meanwhile, combine the broth and tomatoes in a large saucepan. Bring to a boil, then reduce the heat to low and simmer, uncovered, for 5 minutes. Add the beans and vinegar, and return to a simmer.

Drain the pasta in a colander, and stir it into the soup. Simmer 1 minute. Remove from heat, and stir in the pesto. Ladle soup into bowls, and top with croutons, if desired.

Makes 4 servings

> **Per Serving:**
> 277 Calories; 13g Protein; 7g Fat;
> 47g Carbohydrates; 2mg Cholesterol; 1,181mg Sodium; 8g Fiber.

Tortellini and Yellow Squash in Garlic Broth

*Don't be afraid of the garlic in this recipe: The taste mellows
as it simmers into a nutty-sweet flavor.*

1 cup vegetable broth
18 cloves garlic, peeled and
    halved (see Helpful Hint)
One 9-ounce package refriger-
    ated light or regular cheese
    tortellini
3½ cups (about 1 pound) baby
    pattypan and yellow
    pattypan squash, halved, or
    ¾-inch chunks of zucchini
    and yellow squash
Freshly ground black pepper
Freshly grated Parmesan
    cheese (optional)

Combine the broth and garlic in a small saucepan. Cover, and bring to a boil over high heat. Reduce the heat, and simmer, covered, until the garlic is very tender, about 12 minutes.

Meanwhile, in a large saucepan, bring 3 quarts of water to a boil. Place the tortellini in the boiling water, stir, and return to a boil. Cook, stirring occasionally, until al dente, 6 to 8 minutes, adding the squash during the last 3 minutes of cooking.

Pour the garlic and the broth into a blender or food processor, and process until smooth. Drain the tortellini and squash, and transfer it to a large serving bowl. Add the garlic puree and toss. Sprinkle with pepper to taste, and serve with cheese, if desired.

Makes 3 to 4 servings

Helpful Hint

To peel garlic quickly and easily, trim both ends of the cloves and cut them in half lengthwise. The skins should slip right off, but if they don't, whack them with the flat side of a chef's knife or the bottom of a heavy glass or jar to crush the clove and separate it from the peel.

Per Serving:
354 Calories; 16g Protein; 7g Fat; 59g Carbohydrates; 45mg Cholesterol; 669mg Sodium; 8g Fiber.

Tomato Rotini with White Beans and Escarole

A delicious, Tuscan-style peasant dish.

8 ounces tomato or sun-dried
  tomato rotini or penne
1 tablespoon olive oil
4 cloves garlic, minced
1 tablespoon all-purpose flour
One 14½-ounce can vegetable
  broth
One 16- to 19-ounce can
  cannellini or great Northern
  beans, rinsed and drained
4 cups packed (5 ounces) torn
  escarole or spinach leaves
½ cup (2 ounces) freshly grated
  Asiago cheese
Freshly ground black pepper

In a large saucepan, bring 3 quarts of water to a boil. Place the pasta in the boiling water, stir, and return to a boil. Cook, stirring occasionally, until al dente, 8 to 10 minutes.

Meanwhile, heat the oil over medium heat in a large, deep skillet. Add the garlic, and cook, stirring, for 2 minutes. Add the flour, and cook, stirring, 1 minute. Stir in the broth and bring to a boil over medium-high heat, stirring frequently. Add the beans and escarole or spinach, and cook until the greens are wilted, about 3 minutes.

Drain the pasta in a colander, and add it to the skillet with the bean mixture. Cook 2 minutes, stirring occasionally. Transfer to shallow bowls. Top with cheese and serve with pepper.

Makes 4 servings

Per Serving:
341 Calories; 17g Protein; 8g Fat; 61g Carbohydrates; 5mg Cholesterol; 949mg Sodium; 15g Fiber.

67

Alphabet Vegetable Soup

Homemade alphabet soup can be made in minutes with frozen soup vegetables and canned broth.

Two 14½-ounce cans vegetable broth
2 cups water
¾ cup (4 ounces) tricolor or regular small alphabet pasta
One 16-ounce package frozen soup vegetables with potatoes, carrots, peas, etc.
¾ teaspoon dried thyme
¼ teaspoon salt, or to taste
¼ teaspoon freshly ground black pepper
Garlic croutons (optional)

Bring the broth and water to a boil in a large saucepan. Stir in the pasta, reduce the heat to low, and simmer, uncovered, for 4 minutes.

Meanwhile, thaw the vegetables in the microwave oven on high power for about 3 minutes, or under warm running tap water.

Add the vegetables, thyme, salt, and pepper to the broth and simmer, uncovered, for 5 minutes. Ladle into soup bowls, and sprinkle with croutons, if desired.

Makes 4 servings

Per Serving:
193 Calories; 8g Protein; 1g Fat;
40g Carbohydrates; 0 Cholesterol;
615mg Sodium; 6g Fiber.

Caramelized Onion and Swiss Chard Stew

*Corn pasta, available in supermarkets and natural food stores,
is a real boon for those allergic to wheat.*

8 ounces corn or whole wheat gemelli pasta
1 tablespoon butter
1 large or 2 medium yellow or other sweet onions, thinly sliced, separated into rings
⅓ cup cider vinegar
2 tablespoons honey or 1 tablespoon granulated sugar
½ teaspoon paprika
½ teaspoon salt
¼ teaspoon freshly ground black pepper
6 cups (1 large bunch, about 12 ounces) coarsely chopped Swiss chard or kale
½ cup vegetable broth
1 teaspoon cornstarch
½ cup grated Emmentaler (see Helpful Hint) or Swiss cheese (optional)

In a large saucepan, bring 3 quarts of water to a boil. Place the pasta in the boiling water, stir, and return to a boil. Cook, stirring occasionally, until al dente, 8 to 10 minutes.

Meanwhile, melt the butter in a large skillet over medium-high heat. Add the onion rings, cover, and cook 1 minute. Remove the cover, and reduce the heat to medium-low. Cook until tender, stirring occasionally, 7 to 8 minutes.

Add the vinegar, honey or sugar, paprika, salt, and pepper to the skillet with the onions; cook 6 minutes, stirring occasionally. Add the Swiss chard or kale, increase the heat to medium-high, cover, and simmer greens until wilted, about 2 minutes.

Meanwhile, in a cup, combine the broth and cornstarch, and mix well. Add the cornstarch mixture to the skillet and simmer, uncovered, until the sauce thickens, about 2 minutes.

Drain the pasta and transfer it to a serving bowl or platter. Add the onion mixture and toss. Sprinkle with cheese, if desired.

Makes 4 servings

Helpful Hint

Emmentaler cheese is a Swiss cheese (from the Emmental valley) with a distinctive nutty flavor and golden color.

Per Serving:
276 Calories; 6g Protein; 4g Fat; 57g Carbohydrates; 8mg Cholesterol; 564mg Sodium; 9g Fiber.

Radiatore with Limas and Romano

8 ounces tricolored, whole wheat, or regular radiatore pasta
1 tablespoon butter
1 medium yellow or other sweet onion, chopped
4 cloves garlic, minced
1 teaspoon all-purpose flour
One 10-ounce package baby lima beans, thawed
¾ cup vegetable broth
1 tablespoon chopped fresh rosemary or 1 teaspoon dried, crushed
¼ teaspoon salt, or to taste
¼ teaspoon freshly ground black pepper
1 cup diced yellow tomato or halved yellow cherry tomatoes or small roma tomatoes
½ cup (2 ounces) shaved or grated Romano cheese

In a large saucepan, bring 3 quarts of water to a boil. Place the pasta in the boiling water, stir, and return to a boil. Cook, stirring occasionally, until al dente, 8 to 10 minutes.

Meanwhile, melt the butter in a large skillet over medium heat. Add the onion, and cook, stirring, 5 minutes. Add the garlic, and cook, stirring, 2 minutes more. Sprinkle the flour over the onion and the garlic, and cook 1 minute, stirring frequently.

Add the lima beans, broth, rosemary, salt, and pepper, and simmer 5 minutes, stirring occasionally.

Drain the pasta in a colander, add it to the skillet with the bean mixture, and toss well. Transfer to serving plates; top with tomato and cheese.

Makes 4 servings

Per Serving:
347 Calories; 15g Protein; 8g Fat; 54g Carbohydrates; 21mg Cholesterol; 579mg Sodium; 7g Fiber.

Somen Lo Mein

Somen noodles are very thin noodles sold in Asian markets, natural food stores, and some supermarkets. If they are not available, substitute capellini.

8 ounces somen noodles
1 tablespoon peanut or vegetable oil
3 cups sliced Chinese or napa cabbage
4 cloves garlic, minced
2 teaspoons minced fresh gingerroot
One 16-ounce package frozen Oriental or stir-fry vegetables, thawed
½ cup vegetable broth or pasta cooking water
⅓ cup white or other "mellow" miso
½ teaspoon red pepper flakes
2 teaspoons sesame seeds, toasted (optional; see Helpful Hint)

In a large saucepan, bring 3 quarts of water to a boil. Place the noodles in the boiling water, stir, and return to a boil. Cook, stirring occasionally, until al dente, about 2 minutes.

Meanwhile, heat the oil in a large nonstick skillet over medium-high heat. Add the cabbage, garlic, and ginger, and cook, stirring, for 1 minute. Add the thawed vegetables, broth or water, miso, and pepper flakes, and simmer until the vegetables are crisp-tender, 3 to 4 minutes.

Drain the noodles, and transfer to a large bowl or serving platter. Add the vegetable mixture, and toss well. Sprinkle with sesame seeds, if desired.

Makes 6 servings

Helpful Hint

It takes only a minute or two to toast seeds or nuts. Pour them into a dry, nonstick skillet and heat over medium heat, stirring or shaking the pan constantly to avoid burning. Remove the seeds from the skillet immediately after toasting.

Per Serving:
220 Calories; 8g Protein; 4g Fat; 39g Carbohydrates; 0 Cholesterol; 1,355mg Sodium; 5g Fiber.

Fried Tofu with Chutney-Lime Pasta

Three different types of pasta work well in this hearty dish redolent in the Asian flavors of chutney, lime, ginger, and peanuts.

8 ounces whole wheat or regular mostaccioli, gemelli, or ziti

8 ounces snow peas, trimmed (halved if large)

1 red or orange bell pepper, cut into short, thin strips

One 10½-ounce package low-fat, extra-firm tofu

2 tablespoons tamari or soy sauce

1 tablespoon cornmeal

Nonstick cooking spray

¼ cup bottled mango chutney (large pieces of mango chopped)

1 tablespoon peanut or vegetable oil

1 tablespoon fresh lime juice

1 teaspoon bottled minced fresh gingerroot

In a large saucepan, bring 3 quarts of water to a boil. Place the pasta in the boiling water, stir, and return to a boil. Cook, stirring occasionally, until al dente, 8 to 10 minutes, adding snow peas and bell pepper during last 2 to 3 minutes of cooking time.

Meanwhile, drain the tofu and pat dry with a paper towel. Cut the tofu into 1-inch cubes, and place them in a medium bowl. Sprinkle the tofu with 1 tablespoon of the tamari or soy sauce; toss gently to coat. Sprinkle with cornmeal and toss again, gently. Heat a large nonstick skillet over medium heat until hot. Coat with cooking spray. Add the tofu, and cook 3 minutes, turning once.

In a large bowl, combine the chutney, remaining 1 tablespoon tamari or soy sauce, oil, lime juice, and ginger, and mix well. Drain the pasta and vegetables in a colander, and add them to the chutney mixture; toss well. Transfer to serving plates. Top with fried tofu.

Makes 4 to 6 servings

Per Serving:
349 Calories; 17g Protein; 5g Fat; 63g Carbohydrates; 0 Cholesterol; 716mg Sodium; 2g Fiber.

Black Pepper Fettuccine with Asparagus, Bread Crumbs, and Garlic

An elegant main dish.

12 ounces fresh black-pepper fettuccine or 8 ounces three-pepper fettuccine
3 cups cut asparagus spears (1-inch pieces)
2 medium slices sourdough bread
2 tablespoons extra-virgin olive oil
4 cloves garlic, very thinly sliced
½ cup vegetable broth
¼ cup chopped fresh basil or parsley
½ cup freshly grated Parmesan cheese (optional)

In a large saucepan, bring 3 quarts of water to a boil. Place the fettuccine in the boiling water, stir, and return to a boil. Cook, stirring occasionally, until al dente, 8 to 10 minutes, adding asparagus to cooking water during last 2 minutes.

Meanwhile, break the bread into chunks, and place them in a food processor fitted with a steel blade. Process into coarse crumbs.

(You should have about 1 cup bread crumbs.)

Heat 1 tablespoon of the oil in a large nonstick skillet over medium heat. Add the garlic, and cook, stirring, 2 minutes (do not brown). Add the bread crumbs, and cook, stirring, until the garlic and bread crumbs are golden brown, about 6 minutes more.

Drain the pasta and asparagus in a colander and set aside.

Add the broth and the remaining 1 tablespoon oil to the pasta cooking pot; cook over medium heat until simmering, about 1 minute. Return the pasta and asparagus to the cooking pot with the broth; toss well. Transfer to serving plates; sprinkle with basil or parsley, bread crumb mixture, and cheese, if desired.

Makes 6 servings

VARIATION

Substitute green beans for the asparagus. Add to the cooking water during last 4 minutes of pasta cooking time.

Per Serving:
316 Calories; 11g Protein; 8g Fat; 52g Carbohydrates; 0 Cholesterol; 155mg Sodium; 3g Fiber.

73

Tofu with Lemongrass and Soba Noodles

Lemongrass, also called lemongrass hearts and a staple of Thai cuisine, is available in Asian groceries and in many supermarket produce or canned food sections.

8 ounces soba or udon noodles
One 10½-ounce package low-fat extra-firm tofu
3 tablespoons tamari, low-sodium tamari, or regular soy sauce
2 bottles lemongrass hearts, drained and minced (about ¼ cup), or ¼ cup minced fresh lemongrass
1 tablespoon dark or "toasted" sesame oil
2 teaspoons fresh minced gingerroot
4 cloves garlic, minced
2 cups sliced fresh spinach leaves
1 cup fresh or drained canned bean sprouts
¼ cup crushed peanuts (optional)

In a large saucepan, bring 3 quarts of water to a boil. Place the noodles in the boiling water, stir, and return to a boil. Cook, stirring occasionally, until al dente, about 6 minutes.

Meanwhile, drain the tofu and pat dry with a paper towel. Cut into ³/₄-inch cubes. Transfer the tofu cubes to a medium bowl. Add the tamari or soy sauce; toss lightly and let stand 10 minutes.

Combine the lemongrass, oil, ginger, and garlic in a large bowl. Drain the noodles, add them to the lemongrass mixture, and toss well.

Add the spinach and bean sprouts and toss again. Add the tofu and any remaining liquid from the bowl; toss lightly. Sprinkle with peanuts, if desired.

Makes 4 servings

Per Serving:
303 Calories; 14g Protein; 6g Fat; 49g Carbohydrates; 0 Cholesterol; 880mg Sodium; 5g Fiber.

Rigatoni Ragout

8 ounces rigatoni or
   mostaccioli
2 tablespoons butter
4 cloves garlic, minced
1 tablespoon all-purpose flour
One 14½-ounce can vegetable
   broth
One 16-ounce package frozen
   vegetables with potatoes,
   carrots, onions, and celery
1 teaspoon dried herbes de
   Provence or thyme
½ teaspoon ground sage
½ teaspoon salt, or to taste
¼ teaspoon freshly ground
   black pepper
¼ cup freshly grated Parmesan
   cheese (optional)

In a large saucepan, bring 3 quarts of water to a boil. Place the pasta in the boiling water, stir, and return to a boil. Cook, stirring occasionally, until al dente, 8 to 10 minutes.

Meanwhile, melt the butter in a large saucepan over medium heat. Add the garlic, and cook, stirring, 1 minute. Sprinkle the flour over the garlic, and cook, stirring, 1 minute more. Add the broth, and bring to a boil, stirring frequently.

Add the frozen vegetables, and return to a boil. Stir in the herbes de Provence or thyme, sage, salt, and pepper; simmer uncovered 10 minutes.

Drain the pasta in a colander, and add it to the saucepan with the vegetables; heat through. Ladle into shallow soup bowls, and top with cheese, if desired.

Makes 4 servings

Per Serving:
295 Calories; 10g Protein; 8g Fat; 51g Carbohydrates; 16mg Cholesterol; 819mg Sodium; 8g Fiber.

Provençal Soup with Tomato Pistou

Also called soupe au pistou, this hearty Provençal-style vegetable soup is a cousin to Italian minestrone. Pistou (pesto) is an herbal paste of basil, garlic, and cheese swirled into the soup at the finish. For this lighter, salsa-like version, tomatoes replace the olive oil.

FOR THE SOUP:

2 teaspoons canola oil
1 medium yellow onion, diced
2 stalks celery, sliced
6 cups vegetable broth or
   water
2 cups diced white potatoes
   (peeled if desired)
1 teaspoon herbes de Provence
1 teaspoon salt
½ teaspoon white pepper
4 ounces green beans, trimmed
   and cut into 1-inch sections
½ cup acini di peppe or
   conchigliette piccole

FOR THE TOMATO PISTOU:

2 ripe tomatoes, finely chopped
4 cloves garlic, minced
½ cup basil leaves, coarsely
   chopped
¼ cup freshly grated Parmesan
   cheese

In a large saucepan, heat the oil over medium-high heat. Add the onion and celery and cook, stirring, for 6 to 7 minutes. Add the vegetable broth or water, potatoes, herbs, salt, and pepper, and bring to a simmer. Cook for 10 minutes over medium heat, stirring occasionally.

Add the green beans and pasta and cook for about 15 minutes more, stirring occasionally. Remove from the heat and let stand for 5 minutes.

Meanwhile, in a small mixing bowl, combine the pistou ingredients, and transfer to a serving bowl.

When the soup is ready, ladle into bowls and swirl a heaping tablespoon of pistou into each bowl. Serve with French bread.

Makes 6 servings

Per Serving:
131 Calories; 5g Protein; 3g Fat; 24g Carbohydrates; 0 Cholesterol; 1,402mg Sodium; 2g Fiber.

VARIATIONS

Try parsnips in place of potatoes, or white beans or chopped spinach in place of green beans.

"Rasta Pasta" with Island Pumpkin Sauce

*This island-inspired dish of pasta, pumpkin sauce,
and aromatic tropical spices is sure to please!*

1 tablespoon canola oil
1 medium yellow onion, diced
**1 red bell pepper, seeded and
    diced**
2 cloves garlic, minced
**1 hot chili pepper (such as
    jalapeño or serrano),
    seeded and minced**
One 15-ounce can of pumpkin
2 cups water
**1 cup cooked pinto beans or ¼
    pound extra-firm tofu, diced**
1 teaspoon curry powder
1 teaspoon ground coriander
**½ teaspoon freshly ground
    black pepper**
½ teaspoon salt
¼ teaspoon ground cloves
1 cup low-fat milk or soy milk
1½ pounds ravioli
**¼ cup chopped fresh parsley
    (for garnishing)**

In a large saucepan, heat the oil over medium heat. Add the onion, bell pepper, garlic, and chili and cook, stirring, for 5 minutes.

Add the pumpkin, water, beans or tofu, curry, coriander, pepper, salt, and cloves, and cook for about 15 minutes, stirring occasionally. Stir in the milk and return to a gentle simmer.

Meanwhile, in a large saucepan, bring 5 quarts of water to a boil over medium-high heat. Place the ravioli in the boiling water, stir, and return to a boil. Cook for 12 to 15 minutes until al dente, stirring occasionally. Drain in a colander.

Place the pasta on warm serving plates. Ladle the sauce over the top and sprinkle with parsley.

Makes 6 servings

Per Serving:
250 Calories; 13g Protein; 6g Fat; 26g Carbohydrates; 12mg Cholesterol; 381mg Sodium; 4g Fiber.

Linguine with Herb-Roasted Sweet Peppers and Goat Cheese

A little goat cheese goes a long way. It has a distinctive farmhouse flavor and velvety texture and clings to the pasta almost like a sauce. It combines nicely with roasted bell peppers, herbs, and linguine.

8 ounces linguine
2 red bell peppers
2 green bell peppers
2 tablespoons olive oil
2 tablespoons balsamic vinegar
1 teaspoon Dijon mustard
2 cloves garlic, minced
1 teaspoon dried oregano
½ teaspoon thyme
½ teaspoon basil
½ teaspoon freshly ground black pepper
½ teaspoon salt
1 to 2 ounces smooth goat cheese (chèvre)
¼ cup chopped fresh parsley

In a large saucepan, bring 4 quarts of water to a boil over medium-high heat. Place the linguine in the boiling water, stir, and return to a boil. Cook until al dente, 8 to 10 minutes, stirring occasionally.

Meanwhile, preheat the broiler. Arrange the peppers on a large baking pan. Place the pan beneath the broiler and broil until the peppers are slightly charred and tender (but not burned), 6 to 8 minutes per side. Turn the peppers at least once while they cook.

Remove the peppers from the oven and let cool slightly. Cut out the pepper's inner cores and seeds and discard. With a knife, trim any charred or flaky parts. Cut the flesh into thin strips, julienne-style.

Meanwhile, in a medium mixing bowl, whisk together the oil, vinegar, mustard, garlic, oregano, thyme, basil, pepper, and salt. Add the roasted peppers to the dressing and toss to coat thoroughly. Set aside for 5 to 10 minutes.

Drain the pasta in a colander. In a large serving bowl, combine the pasta and marinated peppers. Gently fold in the goat cheese. Top with the parsley and serve at once.

Makes 4 servings

Per Serving:
305 Calories; 10g Protein; 6g Fat; 54g Carbohydrates; 3mg Cholesterol; 38mg Sodium; 5g Fiber.

Pasta with Sun-Dried Tomatoes and Vegetables

The growing availability (and affordability) of sun-dried tomatoes has expanded the culinary possibilities for this once esoteric ingredient. Sun-dried tomatoes meld well with vinegar, garlic, herbs, and a touch of feta cheese.

½ **cup sun-dried tomatoes (not oil-packed variety)**
3 **tablespoons red wine vinegar**
1 **tablespoon olive or canola oil**
2 **cloves garlic, minced**
1 **teaspoon dried oregano**
½ **teaspoon thyme**
½ **teaspoon freshly ground black pepper**
8 to 10 **broccoli florets, blanched**
½ **cup diced, bottled, roasted sweet bell peppers**
2 to 3 **pepperoncini peppers, seeded and diced**
8 **ounces orecchiette or medium shells**
2 **ounces feta cheese, crumbled**
¼ **cup chopped fresh parsley**

In a medium saucepan, bring 1 quart of water to a boil. Place the sun-dried tomatoes in the boiling water and cook for 2 minutes over medium heat. Drain the tomatoes in a colander and finely chop.

In a medium mixing bowl, whisk together the vinegar, oil, garlic, oregano, thyme, and black pepper. Add the sun-dried tomatoes, broccoli, roasted peppers, and pepperoncinis to the dressing and toss thoroughly. Set aside for 5 to 10 minutes.

Meanwhile, in a large saucepan, bring 4 quarts of water to a boil over medium-high heat. Place the pasta in the boiling water, stir, and return to a boil. Cook until al dente, 8 to 10 minutes, stirring occasionally. Drain in a colander.

In a large serving bowl, combine the pasta with the marinated vegetables. Gently fold in the feta cheese. Top with the parsley and serve immediately.

Makes 4 servings

Per Serving:
256 Calories; 9g Protein; 7g Fat; 40g Carbohydrates; 13mg Cholesterol; 529mg Sodium; 4g Fiber.

Pasta with Tunisian Roasted Vegetables

For this creation, spaghetti and roasted vegetables are tossed together and dressed with a Tunisian-style dressing of lemon, olive oil, cumin, and capers.

2 red or green bell peppers, cored
1 zucchini, halved crosswise and quartered
1 red onion, quartered
4 portabello mushroom caps
2 tablespoons olive oil
Juice of 2 lemons
2 cloves garlic, minced
2 tablespoons minced fresh parsley
1 tablespoon capers, rinsed and drained (see Helpful Hint)
½ teaspoon ground cumin
¼ teaspoon cayenne pepper
12 ounces spaghetti

Preheat the oven to 400°F.

Arrange the peppers, zucchini, onion, and mushrooms on a large sheet pan. Roast for 20 minutes until the vegetables are tender. Using tongs, occasionally turn the vegetables as they cook. Remove the vegetables from the oven and let cool slightly. Place on a cutting board and coarsely chop or julienne.

In a large mixing bowl, combine the olive oil, lemon juice, garlic, parsley, capers, cumin, and cayenne. Add the vegetables to the lemon dressing and set aside for 10 minutes.

Meanwhile, in a large saucepan, bring 4 quarts of water to a boil over medium-high heat. Place the pasta in the boiling water, stir, and return to a boil. Cook until al dente, 8 to 10 minutes, stirring occasionally. Drain in a colander.

Transfer the spaghetti to the lemony vegetable mixture and toss thoroughly. Serve immediately.

Makes 6 servings

Helpful Hint

Capers are the tiny, berrylike buds of a Mediterranean bush, used as a flavoring and as a condiment. Look for them in the pickled vegetable aisle of the supermarket.

Per Serving:
299 Calories; 14g Protein; 6g Fat; 49g Carbohydrates; 0 Cholesterol; 82mg Sodium; 11g Fiber.

M-a-a-arvelous Macaroni Chili

Chili and macaroni, two all-American staples, team up for a hearty "down home" meal brimming with comforting flavors and textures.

1 cup elbow macaroni
2 teaspoons canola oil
1 medium yellow onion, diced
1 green bell pepper, seeded and
  diced
2 stalks celery, diced
3 to 4 cloves garlic, minced
One 28-ounce can stewed
  tomatoes, undrained
One 15-ounce can red kidney
  beans, drained
One 11-ounce can corn kernels,
  drained (about 1 cup)
1 ½ tablespoons chili powder
2 teaspoons dried oregano
1 teaspoon ground cumin
½ teaspoon freshly ground
  black pepper
½ teaspoon salt

In a medium saucepan, bring 3 quarts of water to a boil over medium-high heat. Place the macaroni in the boiling water, stir, and return to a boil. Cook until al dente, about 6 minutes, stirring occasionally. Drain in a colander.

Meanwhile, in a large saucepan, heat the oil over medium-high heat. Add the onion, bell pepper, celery, and garlic and cook, stirring, for 7 minutes. Stir in all of the remaining ingredients, and bring to a simmer. Cook over medium-low heat for 15 minutes, stirring occasionally. Blend in the cooked macaroni and cook for 5 minutes more over low heat. Remove from the heat and let stand for 5 to 10 minutes before serving.

Ladle into bowls and serve with warm corn bread.

Makes 6 servings

Per Serving:
226 Calories; 9g Protein; 3g Fat;
44g Carbohydrates; 0 Cholesterol;
843mg Sodium; 7g Fiber.

Macaroni Noodle Casserole

*This medley of vegetables and elbow macaroni is a light alternative to
traditional casseroles that tend to be gooey, creamy, and loaded with fat.
The trick is use low-fat milk and thicken it with cornstarch.*

2 cups elbow macaroni
2 tablespoons cornstarch
2 tablespoons cold water
2 teaspoons canola oil
1 medium yellow onion, diced
**8 ounces button mushrooms,
     sliced**
2 cloves garlic, minced
2 cups low-fat milk
2 cups frozen mixed vegetables
**½ teaspoon freshly ground
     black pepper**
½ teaspoon salt
**¼ cup bread crumbs
     (preferably seasoned)**
**½ cup shredded low-fat Swiss
     cheese (optional)**

Preheat the oven to 400°F.

In a medium saucepan, bring 4
quarts of water to a boil over
medium-high heat. Place the
macaroni in the boiling water, stir,
and return to a boil. Cook until al
dente, about 6 minutes, stirring
occasionally. Drain in a colander.

In a small mixing bowl, stir the
cornstarch and water together
until smooth. Set aside.

Meanwhile, in a large saucepan,
heat the oil over medium-high
heat. Add the onion, mushrooms,
and garlic and cook, stirring, for 5
minutes. Stir in the milk, mixed
vegetables, pepper, and salt, and
bring to a gentle simmer over
medium heat. Whisk in the
cornstarch mixture. Fold in the
macaroni. Ladle the entire mixture
into a 9½-inch × 13-inch casserole
and sprinkle with bread crumbs
and cheese (if desired). Bake until
bubbly, 5 to 7 minutes.

Remove from the oven and
let stand for 5 minutes before
serving.

Makes 4 servings

Per Serving:
389 Calories; 16g Protein; 5g Fat;
71g Carbohydrates; 5mg Cholesterol; 450mg Sodium; 8g Fiber.

Pasta Pronto with Greens and Beans

This dish meets the four basic requirements of the working family's household: It is simple, nourishing, tasty (of course), and, most of all, quick!

1 tablespoon olive oil
1 medium yellow onion, diced
2 cloves garlic, minced
One 6-ounce can tomato paste
2 cups water
1 teaspoon dried basil
½ teaspoon freshly ground
    black pepper
½ teaspoon salt
4 cups coarsely chopped
    spinach
One 15-ounce can chickpeas,
    drained
8 ounces spaghetti or linguine
¼ cup chopped fresh parsley

In a medium saucepan, heat the oil over medium heat. Add the onion and garlic and cook, stirring, for 4 minutes. Blend in the tomato paste, water, basil, pepper, and salt, and stir to form a sauce.

Stir in the spinach. Cook, uncovered, over medium-low heat for 5 to 7 minutes, stirring occasionally.

Stir in the chickpeas and cook for 5 minutes more over low heat, stirring occasionally.

Meanwhile, in a large saucepan, bring 3 quarts of water to a boil over medium-high heat. Place the pasta in the boiling water, stir, and return to a boil. Cook until al dente, 8 to 10 minutes, stirring occasionally. Drain in a colander.

Transfer the pasta to warm serving plates. Ladle the tomato sauce over the pasta and sprinkle with parsley.

Makes 4 servings

Per Serving:
412 Calories; 16g Protein; 6g Fat;
75g Carbohydrates; 0 Cholesterol;
665mg Sodium; 10g Fiber.

Warm Penne with Asparagus and Citrus Vinaigrette

Asparagus spears and penne, both narrow and pencil-shaped, complement each other nicely when tossed together. A zesty dressing of lemon and lime seals the deal.

8 ounces penne
10 to 12 fresh asparagus spears, trimmed and cut into 1-inch pieces
½ cup bottled, roasted sweet peppers, cut into thin strips
3 to 4 whole scallions, trimmed and chopped
Juice of 1 lemon
Juice of 1 lime
2 tablespoons olive oil
2 cloves garlic, minced
2 tablespoons chopped fresh parsley
½ teaspoon freshly ground black pepper
½ teaspoon salt

In a large saucepan, bring 3 quarts of water to a boil over medium-high heat. Place the penne in the boiling water, stir, and return to a boil. Cook for 5 minutes, stirring occasionally. Add the asparagus to the pan, stir, and continue cooking until the pasta is al dente, 4 to 6 minutes more, stirring occasionally. Drain the pasta and asparagus in a colander.

Meanwhile, in a large mixing bowl, combine all of the remaining ingredients. Fold in the pasta and asparagus and toss to coat. Serve warm.

Makes 4 servings

VARIATION

Add other vegetables, such as one 14-ounce can of artichokes, ¼ pound of green beans, or a small bunch of kale.

Per Serving:
234 Calories; 6g Protein; 8g Fat; 35g Carbohydrates; 0 Cholesterol; 299mg Sodium; 3g Fiber.

"Campfire Pasta" with Grilled Vegetables

The words pasta and grilling are not commonly used in the same sentence, but that shouldn't stop the adventurous cook. Lightly grilled vegetables can imbue pasta with a smoky, but not overpowering, essence.

2 tablespoons olive oil
2 tablespoons red wine vinegar
2 tablespoons chopped fresh
  parsley
1 teaspoon dried oregano
¼ teaspoon cayenne pepper
½ teaspoon salt
1 zucchini or yellow squash,
  quartered lengthwise
1 medium red onion, quartered
1 red bell pepper, cored
3 to 4 portabello mushroom
  caps
8 ounces linguine or spaghetti

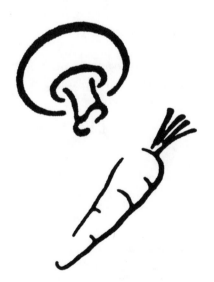

Preheat the grill until the coals are gray to white.

In a large mixing bowl, combine the olive oil, vinegar, parsley, oregano, cayenne, and salt. Set aside.

When the fire is ready, arrange the vegetables on the grill. Cook until the vegetables are tender, about 5 minutes on each side. Transfer the vegetables to a cutting board, let cool slightly, and coarsely chop. Toss the vegetables with the vinaigrette mixture.

Meanwhile, in a large saucepan, bring 3 quarts of water to a boil over medium-high heat. Place the pasta in the boiling water, stir, and return to a boil. Cook until al dente, 8 to 10 minutes, stirring occasionally. Drain in a colander.

Add the pasta to the grilled vegetable mixture and toss together. Serve with warm garlic bread.

Makes 4 servings

Per Serving:
253 Calories; 7g Protein; 8g Fat;
40g Carbohydrates; 0 Cholesterol;
299mg Sodium; 5g Fiber.

Sesame Soba Noodles with Asian Flavors

This dish of sesame-scented pasta is a harmonious blend of crunchy snow peas and scallions, firm mushrooms, tender noodles, and tofu. Sesame oil, soy sauce, and rice vinegar strike a happy medium.

8 ounces soba (buckwheat) or somen noodles
2 teaspoons peanut oil
1 red or yellow bell pepper, seeded and cut into ¼-inch-wide matchsticks
6 to 8 fresh shiitake mushrooms, halved
2 teaspoons minced fresh gingerroot
4 whole scallions, trimmed and chopped
4 ounces whole snow peas, trimmed
4 ounces extra-firm tofu, cut into ¼-inch-wide matchsticks
2 tablespoons low-sodium soy sauce
1 tablespoon sesame oil
1 tablespoon rice vinegar

In a large saucepan, bring 3 quarts of water to a boil over medium-high heat. Place the noodles in boiling water and cook until al dente, 4 to 5 minutes, stirring occasionally. Drain in a colander.

Meanwhile, in a large wok or skillet, heat the peanut oil over medium-high heat. Add the bell pepper, mushrooms, and ginger and cook, stirring, for 3 to 4 minutes. Stir in the scallions, snow peas, and tofu and cook, stirring, for 3 to 4 minutes more. Stir in the soy sauce, sesame oil, and rice vinegar and bring to a simmer. Cook, stirring, for 2 minutes. Fold in the cooked noodles.

Spoon the vegetable and noodle mixture onto warm plates and serve immediately.

Makes 4 servings

Per Serving:
325 Calories; 11g Protein; 9g Fat; 51g Carbohydrates; 0 Cholesterol; 406mg Sodium; 5g Fiber.

Linguine with Wild Mushroom Alfredo

Here is vivid proof that a luscious white sauce does not have to contain full-fat heavy cream, eggs, or gobs of butter. For this improvisation of a classic Alfredo, a trio of mushrooms provides an appetizing foundation for a light but enriching sauce.

8 ounces linguine
1 tablespoon olive oil or canola oil
1 tablespoon dry white wine
8 ounces button mushrooms, sliced
6 to 8 fresh shiitake mushrooms, sliced
4 ounces oyster mushrooms, sliced
3 to 4 cloves garlic, minced
2 cups low-fat milk
2 tablespoons chopped fresh parsley
1½ tablespoons Dijon mustard
½ teaspoon dried thyme
½ teaspoon white pepper
½ teaspoon salt
2 tablespoons cornstarch
2 tablespoons cold water

In a large saucepan, bring 3 quarts of water to a boil over medium-high heat. Place the linguine in the boiling water, stir, and return to a boil. Cook until al dente, 8 to 10 minutes, stirring occasionally. Drain the linguine in a colander.

In another large saucepan, heat the oil and wine over medium-high heat. Add the mushrooms and garlic and cook, stirring, for 6 to 8 minutes. Stir in the milk, parsley, mustard, thyme, pepper, and salt, and bring to a gentle simmer over medium heat.

Meanwhile, in a small mixing bowl, stir the cornstarch and water until smooth, and stir the mixture into the sauce; return to a gentle simmer. Fold in the cooked linguine. Cook for about 1 minute more over low heat, stirring frequently.

Transfer to warm serving plates and serve immediately.

Makes 4 servings

VARIATION

For a low-sodium version, add the juice of 1 lemon to the sauce a few minutes before serving and omit the salt.

Per Serving:
313 Calories; 13g Protein; 7g Fat; 53g Carbohydrates; 5mg Cholesterol; 393mg Sodium; 5g Fiber.

Vietnamese Pho with Exotic Mushrooms and Tofu

Pho in Vietnamese refers to noodle soup (loosely translated, it means "your own bowl"). The pot resonates with chewy wood ear mushrooms, crunchy snow peas, and sprouts, soft tofu and noodles, and subtle nuances imposed by lime and ginger.

½ ounce dried wood ear mushrooms or dried shiitake
   mushrooms
2 teaspoons peanut oil
1 medium yellow onion, diced
2 teaspoons minced fresh
   gingerroot
5 cups vegetable broth
2 carrots, peeled and thinly
   sliced at an angle
4 ounces whole snow peas,
   trimmed and coarsely
   chopped
4 ounces extra-firm tofu, diced
¼ cup low-sodium soy sauce
½ teaspoon freshly ground
   black pepper
2 tablespoons chopped cilantro
   (optional)
Juice of 1 lime
8 ounces rice noodles

GARNISHES:

2 large whole scallions,
   trimmed and chopped
2 ounces bean sprouts

Per Serving:
217 Calories; 6g Protein; 4g Fat;
42g Carbohydrates; 0 Cholesterol;
1,296mg Sodium; 2g Fiber.

In a small pan or mixing bowl, cover the dried mushrooms with 1 cup boiling water. Set aside for 5 minutes. Drain and coarsely chop the reconstituted mushrooms.

Meanwhile, in a large saucepan, heat the oil over medium-high heat. Add the onion and ginger and cook, stirring, for 3 minutes. Add the vegetable broth, carrots, snow peas, tofu, soy sauce, black pepper, and mushrooms and bring to a simmer. Cook over medium heat for about 10 minutes, stirring occasionally. Stir in the cilantro and lime juice.

Meanwhile, in another large saucepan, bring 3 quarts of water to a boil over medium-high heat. Place the rice noodles in the boiling water, stir, and return to a boil. Cook until al dente, 4 to 5 minutes, stirring occasionally. Drain the noodles in a colander.

Place the cooked noodles into soup bowls. Ladle the pho broth over the noodles. Arrange the scallions and bean sprouts over the top of each bowl.

Makes 6 servings

Cajun Macaroni and Red Beans

The Cajun propensity for piquant flavors and wholesome, unpretentious portions comes to fruition in this satisfying tureen of elbow macaroni, beans, and sturdy vegetables.

1 cup elbow macaroni
1 tablespoon canola oil
1 green bell pepper, seeded and diced
1 medium yellow onion, diced
1 stalk celery, diced
2 cloves garlic, minced
One 15-ounce can tomato puree
One 14-ounce can stewed tomatoes
One 15-ounce can small red beans, drained
2 teaspoons dried oregano
½ teaspoon salt
½ teaspoon freshly ground black pepper
¼ teaspoon cayenne pepper
1 to 2 teaspoons bottled hot sauce

In a medium saucepan, bring 3 quarts of water to a boil over medium-high heat. Place the macaroni in the boiling water, stir, and return to a boil. Cook until al dente, about 6 minutes, stirring occasionally. Drain in a colander.

In a large saucepan heat the oil over medium heat. Add the bell pepper, onion, celery, and garlic and cook, stirring, for 7 to 8 minutes. Add all of the remaining ingredients, and cook over medium-low heat for 15 minutes, stirring occasionally. Fold in the macaroni and cook for 5 minutes more over low heat.

Remove the pan from the heat and let stand for 5 minutes before serving. To serve, ladle the chili into shallow bowls.

Makes 4 servings

VARIATION

For a gourmet twist, spelt elbows or corn macaroni can be substituted for semolina macaroni.

Per Serving:
300 Calories; 12g Protein; 4g Fat; 58g Carbohydrates; 0 Cholesterol; 1,540mg Sodium; 10g Fiber.

Vegetarian Pad Thai with Cashews

Patrons of Thai restaurants will recognize the name of this popular Asian noodle dish. Most versions call for crunchy vegetables, rice noodles, cilantro, and chopped nuts. This rendition is embellished with chopped cashews.

8 ounces rice noodles, either rice sticks or rice vermicelli
2 teaspoons peanut oil
1 red bell pepper, seeded and cut into ¼-inch-wide matchsticks
2 cloves garlic, minced
2 large ripe tomatoes, diced
4 ounces whole snow peas, trimmed
4 ounces extra-firm tofu, cut into ¼-inch-wide match sticks
¼ cup low-sodium soy sauce
Juice of 1 lime
2 tablespoons chopped cilantro

GARNISHES:

¼ cup unsalted roasted cashews, chopped
4 whole scallions, trimmed and chopped
2 ounces bean sprouts

In a large saucepan, bring 3 quarts of water to a boil over medium-high heat. Place the noodles in boiling water and cook until al dente, 4 to 5 minutes, stirring occasionally. Drain in a colander.

Meanwhile, in a large wok or skillet heat the peanut oil over medium-high heat. Add the bell pepper and garlic; stir-fry for 4 minutes. Stir in the tomatoes, snow peas, and tofu and stir-fry for 4 minutes more. Stir in the soy sauce and lime juice and bring to a simmer. Cook, stirring, for 2 to 3 minutes more. Fold in the cooked noodles and cilantro.

Spoon the noodle mixture onto warm plates and arrange the cashews, scallions, and bean sprouts around the edge of the noodles.

Makes 4 servings

Per Serving:
300 Calories; 7g Protein; 4g Fat; 59g Carbohydrates; 0 Cholesterol; 693mg Sodium; 3g Fiber.

Orzo Gumbo

With gumbo, anything goes. For this jazzy pasta-lover's version,
orzo is substituted for rice; the result is a tempting
New Orleans version of minestrone.

1 tablespoon canola oil
1 medium yellow onion, diced
1 green or red bell pepper,
    seeded and diced
1 stalk celery, chopped
2 to 3 cloves garlic, minced
5 cups vegetable stock or water
One 14-ounce can stewed
    tomatoes
1 cup chopped okra (optional)
¼ cup tomato paste
2 teaspoons dried oregano
1 teaspoon dried thyme
½ teaspoon freshly ground
    black pepper
½ teaspoon salt
¼ teaspoon cayenne pepper
1 cup orzo

In a large saucepan, heat the oil.
Add the onion, bell pepper,
celery, and garlic and cook,
stirring, for 5 to 7 minutes. Stir
in the vegetable stock or water,
stewed tomatoes, okra (if desired),
tomato paste, oregano, thyme,
black pepper, salt, and cayenne,
and bring to a simmer. Add the
orzo and cook over medium-high
heat for 15 minutes, stirring
occasionally.

Remove the pan from the heat
and let stand for about 5 minutes.
Ladle the gumbo into shallow
soup bowls and serve with wheat
bread or corn bread.

Makes 6 servings

VARIATIONS

Add one 15-ounce can red kidney
beans (drained). For a spicier
version, add a few dashes of bottled
hot sauce or more cayenne pepper
before serving.

Per Serving:
147 Calories; 6g Protein; 3g Fat;
26g Carbohydrates; 0 Cholesterol;
1,182mg Sodium; 2g Fiber.

Fettuccine with Wine-Braised Mushrooms and Escarole

The aroma of mushrooms simmering in white wine and garlic will pervade the kitchen and rouse the appetite. When combined with braised escarole and fettuccine, a simple but delectable meal is born.

2 teaspoons olive oil
3 tablespoons dry white wine (such as Chardonnay)
12 ounces button mushrooms, sliced
2 cloves garlic, minced
1 medium head escarole, cored and coarsely chopped (see Helpful Hint)
½ teaspoon freshly ground black pepper
½ teaspoon salt
12 ounces fettuccine
¼ cup freshly grated Parmesan cheese

In a large saucepan or wok, heat the oil and wine over medium-high heat. Add the mushrooms and garlic and cook until tender, 6 to 7 minutes. Add the escarole, pepper, and salt, and cook, stirring, until the greens are wilted, about 5 minutes.

Meanwhile, in a large saucepan, bring 4 quarts of water to a boil over medium-high heat. Place the pasta in the boiling water, stir, and return to a boil. Cook until al dente, 8 to 10 minutes, stirring occasionally. Drain in a colander.

Fold the fettuccine into the escarole and mushroom mixture. Blend in the cheese and serve immediately.

Makes 4 servings

Helpful Hint

Escarole, an Italian leafy green, has a mild bitter flavor and cooks up quickly, similar to spinach or chard.

Per Serving:
400 Calories; 16g Protein; 6g Fat; 71g Carbohydrates; 4mg Cholesterol; 451mg Sodium; 10g Fiber.

Acini di Peppe with Spinach and Eggs

This dish was inspired by an Italian meal of pasta and eggs, sort of an Italian version of "egg fried rice." For this light interpretation, braised spinach is substituted for about half of the eggs and all of the cheese.

1½ cups acini di peppe (tubettini)
2 teaspoons canola oil
1 medium yellow onion, diced
4 cups coarsely chopped spinach, rinsed and packed
2 large eggs, beaten
½ teaspoon freshly ground black pepper
½ teaspoon salt

In a large saucepan, bring 3 quarts of water to a boil over medium-high heat. Place the pasta in the boiling water, stir, and return to a boil. Cook until al dente, 5 to 7 minutes, stirring occasionally. Drain in a colander.

Meanwhile, in a large saucepan, heat the oil over medium heat. Add the onion and cook, stirring, for 3 minutes. Add the spinach and cook, stirring, until the leaves are wilted, about 4 minutes. Fold in the acini di peppe and all of the remaining ingredients, and cook, stirring, until the eggs are fully cooked and no longer opaque, 2 to 3 minutes. Serve as a side dish or brunch entrée.

Makes 4 servings

Per Serving:
228 Calories; 10g Protein; 7g Fat; 34g Carbohydrates; 106mg Cholesterol; 369mg Sodium; 3g Fiber.

Pasta Fresca with Spicy Winter Greens

*Winter greens radiate spicy, mustardy flavors and rapidly "cook down"
to one-quarter of their original volume (the flavors also become more
concentrated). The quick-cooking greens are paired with fresh pasta,
which also can be ready in minutes. For variety's sake, try a flavored
pasta made with spinach, tomato-basil, or chili peppers.*

1 tablespoon canola oil
3 to 4 cloves garlic, minced
**6 cups coarsely chopped mixed
     winter greens (such as
     mizuna, frisé, arugula, red
     kale, and beet greens; see
     Helpful Hint)**
3 tablespoons balsamic vinegar
**½ teaspoon freshly ground
     black pepper**
12 ounces fresh linguine
**¼ cup freshly grated Parmesan
     cheese**

In large saucepan or wok, heat the
oil over medium heat. Add the
garlic and cook, stirring, until
lightly browned, 2 to 3 minutes.
Reduce the heat to low and add
the mixed greens, vinegar, and
pepper. Cook, stirring, until the
greens are wilted, 3 to 4 minutes.
Remove from the heat.

Meanwhile, in a large saucepan,
bring 4 quarts of water to a boil
over medium-high heat. Place the
linguine in the boiling water,
gently stir, and return to a boil.
Cook until al dente, 4 to 5 minutes, stirring occasionally. Drain
in a colander.

Combine the noodles with the
wilted greens. Fold in the cheese.
Transfer the linguine and greens
to warm plates and serve at once.

Makes 4 servings

Helpful Hint

*Winter greens are actually avail-
able in the winter, spring, and
autumn at farmer's markets,
natural food stores, and well-
stocked supermarkets.*

Per Serving:
349 Calories; 14g Protein; 9g Fat;
55g Carbohydrates; 99mg Cholesterol; 192mg Sodium; 4g Fiber.

Tortellini with Tomato-Curry Sauce

The aromatic presence of curry powder and ginger bring an uplifting flavor to this savory meal of chewy tortellini with red sauce.

1 tablespoon olive oil
1 small yellow onion, diced
2 cloves garlic, minced
2 teaspoons minced fresh
  gingerroot
1 tablespoon dried parsley
1½ teaspoons curry powder
½ teaspoon ground cumin
½ teaspoon salt
¼ teaspoon cayenne pepper
Two 6-ounce cans tomato paste
4 cups water
1 pound dried spinach tortellini
  or cheese tortellini

In a large saucepan, heat the oil over medium heat. Add the onion, garlic, and ginger and cook, stirring, for 3 minutes. Add the parsley, curry, cumin, salt, and cayenne and cook, stirring for 30 seconds. Stir in the tomato paste and water and blend together to form a sauce. Bring to a simmer over medium-high heat, stirring frequently. Reduce the heat to medium-low and cook, uncovered, for 15 to 20 minutes, stirring occasionally.

Meanwhile, in a large saucepan, bring 3 quarts of water to a boil over medium-high heat. Place the tortellini in the boiling water, stir, and return to a boil. Cook until al dente, 12 to 15 minutes, stirring occasionally. Drain the tortellini in a colander.

Transfer the tortellini to warm serving plates and cover with the red curry sauce.

Makes 6 servings

Per Serving:
248 Calories; 12g Protein; 7g Fat; 36g Carbohydrates; 18mg Cholesterol; 419mg Sodium; 3g Fiber.

Perciatelli with Eggplant and Tempeh

Perciatelli refers to long, spaghetti-like noodles pierced with what seems to be narrow air tunnels. The bouncy noodles deserve a robust tomato sauce (this rendition is fortified with chunks of eggplant and tempeh).

1 tablespoon canola oil
1 medium yellow onion, diced
1 red or green bell pepper,
   seeded and diced
2 cups diced eggplant
4 cloves garlic, minced
One 28-ounce can stewed
   tomatoes
One 14-ounce can tomato puree
¼ pound tempeh, diced (see
   Helpful Hint)
1 teaspoon dried oregano
1 teaspoon dried basil
½ teaspoon freshly ground
   black pepper
½ teaspoon salt
1 pound perciatelli, spaghetti,
   or linguine

In a large saucepan, heat the oil over medium-high heat. Add the onion, bell pepper, eggplant, and garlic. Cook, stirring, for 8 to 10 minutes over medium heat. Add the stewed tomatoes, tomato puree, tempeh, oregano, basil, pepper, and salt. Cook for 15 to 20 minutes more, stirring occasionally.

Meanwhile, in a large saucepan, bring 4 quarts of water to a boil over medium-high heat. Place the noodles in the boiling water, stir, and return to a boil. Cook until al dente, 13 to 15 minutes, stirring occasionally. Drain in a colander.

Transfer the noodles to warm serving dishes and ladle the sauce over the top.

Makes 6 servings

Helpful Hint

Tempeh is a chewy meat substitute made with cooked, aged soybeans and grains. It is sold in the refrigerated or produce section of natural food stores and well-stocked supermarkets.

Per Serving:
416 Calories; 16g Protein; 5g Fat;
76g Carbohydrates; 0 Cholesterol;
586mg Sodium; 9g Fiber.

Moo Goo Noodles with Tofu and Mushrooms

Patrons of Chinese restaurants will recognize the term moo goo gai pan. This meatless version combines tofu, mushrooms, and lo mein noodles with traditional Asian flavors.

½ ounce dried exotic mushrooms (such as wood ear, shiitake, or wild lobster)
8 ounces wide lo mein noodles
1 tablespoon peanut oil
1 red bell pepper, seeded and cut into thin strips
4 ounces snow peas, trimmed and halved
4 ounces tofu or tempeh, diced
2 cloves garlic, minced
2 teaspoons minced fresh gingerroot
½ cup vegetable broth
¼ cup low-sodium soy sauce
4 whole scallions, trimmed and chopped
1 tablespoon dark or "toasted" sesame oil

In a small pan or mixing bowl, cover the dried mushrooms with 1 cup boiling water. Set aside for 5 minutes. Drain and coarsely chop the reconstituted mushrooms.

In a large saucepan, bring 3 quarts of water to a boil over medium-high heat. Place the noodles in the boiling water, stir, and return to a boil. Cook until al dente, 4 to 5 minutes, stirring occasionally. Drain the noodles in a colander and briefly rinse under warm water.

Meanwhile, in a large skillet or wok, heat the oil over medium-high heat. Add the bell pepper and snow peas and stir-fry for about 4 minutes. Stir in the tofu or tempeh, garlic, ginger, and mushrooms and stir-fry for 4 minutes more. Stir in the vegetable broth, soy sauce, scallions, and sesame oil and bring to a simmer. Cook, stirring, about 4 minutes. Fold in the cooked lo mein noodles.

Transfer the noodle mixture to warm serving plates and serve at once.

Makes 4 servings

Per Serving:
149 Calories; 6g Protein; 5g Fat; 19g Carbohydrates; 0 Cholesterol; 406mg Sodium; 3g Fiber.

Asian Noodle Stir-Fry with Sun-Dried Tomatoes

This all-purpose stir-fry is a filling dish adorned with herbal flavors. Dried basil delivers a hint of anise and cilantro arrives with its distinctive pungent personality. For optimal results, finely chop the sun-dried tomatoes after rehydrating.

½ cup sun-dried tomatoes
    (not oil-packed)
12 ounces rice vermicelli or thin
    lo mein noodles
1 tablespoon peanut oil
4 ounces extra-firm tofu, diced
4 ounces snow peas, trimmed
4 whole scallions, trimmed and
    chopped
2 cloves garlic, minced
½ cup vegetable broth
1 tablespoon rice vinegar
1 teaspoon dried basil
½ teaspoon freshly ground
    black pepper
½ teaspoon salt
2 tablespoons chopped cilantro

In a medium saucepan, bring 1 quart of water to a boil. Place the sun-dried tomatoes in the boiling water and cook for 2 to 3 minutes over medium heat. Drain the tomatoes in a colander and finely chop.

In a large saucepan, bring 4 quarts of water to a boil over medium-high heat. Place the noodles in the boiling water, stir, and return to a boil. Cook until al dente, 4 to 5 minutes, stirring occasionally. Drain in a colander and briefly rinse under warm running water.

Meanwhile, in a large wok or skillet, heat the peanut oil over medium heat. Add the tofu and cook, stirring, for about 3 minutes. Stir in the sun-dried tomatoes, snow peas, scallions, and garlic and cook, stirring, for 3 minutes more. Add the broth, vinegar, basil, pepper, and salt and bring to a simmer. Cook, stirring, for 2 to 3 minutes more. Fold in the cooked noodles and cilantro. Serve at once.

Per Serving:
418 Calories; 12g Protein; 5g Fat; 71g Carbohydrates; 0 Cholesterol; 631mg Sodium; 5g Fiber.

Makes 4 servings

Perciatelli with Mixed Greens Marinara

Hardy leafy greens add both nutrients and striking mustardy flavors to this comforting noodle dish. A variety of greens can be used in the red sauce; choose whatever is available and smart-looking.

1 tablespoon olive oil
1 medium yellow onion, diced
2 cloves garlic, minced
One 28-ounce can plum
    tomatoes
One 14-ounce can tomato puree
1 teaspoon dried oregano
1 teaspoon dried basil
½ teaspoon freshly ground
    black pepper
½ teaspoon salt
4 cups coarsely chopped mixed
    greens (such as spinach,
    arugula, red kale, and
    mizuna)
1 pound perciatelli, spaghetti,
    or linguine

In a large saucepan, heat the oil over medium heat. Add the onion and garlic and cook, stirring, for 3 minutes. Add the plum tomatoes, tomato puree, oregano, basil, pepper, and salt, and bring to a simmer. Cook for 10 minutes over medium-low heat, stirring occasionally.

As the sauce cooks, break up the plum tomatoes with a spoon. Stir in the mixed greens and cook for 5 to 7 minutes more. Set aside until the noodles are ready.

Meanwhile, in a large saucepan, bring 4 quarts of water to a boil over medium-high heat. Place the noodles in the boiling water, stir, and return to a boil. Cook until al dente, 13 to 15 minutes, stirring occasionally. Drain the noodles in a colander.

Transfer the noodles to warm serving plates and ladle the sauce over the top. Serve immediately.

Makes 6 servings

Per Serving:
183 Calories; 6g Protein; 3g Fat; 33g Carbohydrates; 0 Cholesterol; 760mg Sodium; 5g Fiber.

Ramen-Style Noodles in Spicy Vegetable Broth

Commercially prepared ramen noodle soups are inexpensive and convenient, but many brands are loaded with monosodium glutamate, sodium, and fat. This home-cooked version is intensely flavored, aromatic, and brimming with good-for-you vegetables.

½ ounce dried wild lobster
   mushrooms (see Helpful
   Hints) or other exotic
   mushrooms
5 cups vegetable broth
2 carrots, peeled and thinly
   sliced diagonally
2 cups shredded bok choy
   leaves
1 cup shredded cabbage
¼ pound extra-firm tofu, diced
¼ cup low-sodium soy sauce
2 teaspoons minced fresh
   gingerroot (optional)
2 teaspoons sesame oil
1 teaspoon chili-garlic paste
   (see Helpful Hints)
8 ounces chuka soba (ramen or
   Chinese or Japanese curly
   noodles)
2 large whole scallions,
   trimmed and chopped

In a small pan or mixing bowl, cover the dried mushrooms with 1 cup boiling water. Set aside for 5 minutes. Drain and slice the reconstituted mushrooms.

Meanwhile, in a large saucepan, add the broth, carrots, bok choy, cabbage, tofu, soy sauce, ginger, sesame oil, chili-garlic paste, and mushrooms. Bring to a simmer over medium high heat. Cook for 12 to 15 minutes, stirring occasionally.

Meanwhile, in another large saucepan, bring 4 quarts of water to a boil over medium-high heat. Place the noodles in the boiling water. When the noodles rise to the top, gently stir, and cook until al dente, 4 to 5 minutes, stirring occasionally. Drain the noodles in a colander and briefly rinse under warm running water.

Using tongs, place the cooked noodles in wide soup bowls. Ladle the broth and vegetables over the noodles; shower the scallions over the top.

Makes 4 servings

Per Serving:
176 Calories; 11g Protein; 7g Fat; 21g Carbohydrates; 8mg Cholesterol; 2,091mg Sodium; 3g Fiber.

Helpful Hints

Wild lobster mushrooms are orange-red mushrooms with a taste and texture reminiscent of lobster.

Chili-garlic paste, sometimes called chili paste, is a seasoning made from fermented beans, chili peppers, and other seasonings. It is sold in jars in the Chinese food section of supermarkets.

Stir-Fried Vegetables with Red Sauce

This cross-cultural dish marries the flavors of an Asian stir-fry with a red sauce rooted in Italian cuisine. The sauce is subtly flavored with ginger, garlic, and soy sauce and chock-full of vegetables and tofu.

1 tablespoon canola oil or peanut oil
8 ounces button mushrooms, sliced
1 medium zucchini, diced
4 ounces extra-firm tofu, diced
8 ounces sliced water chestnuts, drained
2 cloves garlic, minced
2 teaspoons minced fresh gingerroot
One 28-ounce can tomato puree
¼ cup low-sodium soy sauce
1 to 2 teaspoons dark or "toasted" sesame oil
4 whole scallions, trimmed and chopped
12 ounces rice sticks or lo mein noodles

In a large wok, heat the oil over medium-high heat. Add the mushrooms and zucchini, and cook, stirring, for about 5 minutes. Add the tofu, water chestnuts, garlic, and ginger, and cook, stirring, for 3 to 4 minutes more.

Stir in the tomato puree, soy sauce, and sesame oil, and bring to a simmer. Reduce the heat to medium-low, and cook for 12 to 15 minutes, stirring frequently. Stir in the scallions.

Meanwhile, in a large saucepan, bring 3 quarts of water to a boil over medium-high heat. Place the noodles in the boiling water, stir, and return to a boil. Cook until al dente, 4 to 5 minutes, stirring occasionally. Drain in a colander and briefly rinse under warm water.

Transfer the noodles to warm serving plates and spoon the red sauce over the top.

Makes 4 servings

VARIATION

If you prefer a thinner sauce, add ¼ to ⅓ cup vegetable broth along with the tomato puree.

Per Serving:
532 Calories; 16g Protein; 7g Fat; 96g Carbohydrates; 0 Cholesterol; 1,412mg Sodium; 12g Fiber.

Rice Vermicelli with African Groundnut Sauce

Groundnut sauce is a rich, nutty sauce of peanut butter, ginger, and tomato paste. This adaptation for pasta includes tofu, bok choy greens, and cilantro.

12 ounces rice vermicelli or rice sticks
2 teaspoons peanut oil
1 small yellow onion, diced
2 teaspoons minced fresh gingerroot
2 cups coarsely chopped bok choy or spinach
¼ pound extra-firm tofu, diced
½ cup water
½ cup peanut butter
2 tablespoons tomato paste
1 tablespoon low-sodium soy sauce
1 teaspoon ground cumin
½ teaspoon freshly ground black pepper
2 tablespoons chopped cilantro

In a large saucepan, bring 3 quarts of water to a boil over medium-high heat. Place the vermicelli in the boiling water, stir, and return to a boil. Cook until al dente, 4 to 5 minutes, stirring occasionally. Drain in a colander.

Meanwhile, in a large wok or skillet, heat the peanut oil over medium heat. Add the onion and ginger and cook, stirring, for 3 minutes. Stir in the bok choy or spinach and tofu and cook, stirring, until the greens are wilted, about 4 minutes. Stir in the water, peanut butter, tomato paste, soy sauce, cumin, and pepper. Cook, stirring, until the sauce is simmering, 2 to 3 minutes more. Fold in the cilantro.

Transfer the noodles to warm plates and ladle the peanut sauce over the top.

Makes 4 servings

Per Serving:
350 Calories; 14g Protein; 12g Fat; 54g Carbohydrates; 0 Cholesterol; 144mg Sodium; 5g Fiber.

Gnocchi with Cabbage and Tomato Sauce

Cabbage is a highly nutritious but often underrated cruciferous vegetable. It adds body and texture to this dish of thick tomato sauce and chewy gnocchi.

1 tablespoon canola oil
1 medium yellow onion, diced
1 green bell pepper, seeded and diced
2 cups coarsely chopped cabbage
2 cloves garlic, minced
One 14-ounce can stewed tomatoes
One 14-ounce can tomato puree
4 ounces green beans, cut into 1-inch sections
2 teaspoons dried oregano
½ teaspoon freshly ground black pepper
¼ teaspoon salt
1 pound frozen gnocchi or cavatelli

In a medium saucepan, heat the oil over medium-high heat. Add the onion, bell pepper, cabbage, and garlic and cook, stirring, for about 6 minutes. Add the stewed tomatoes, tomato puree, green beans, oregano, pepper, and salt, and cook over medium-low heat until the cabbage is tender, about 15 minutes, stirring occasionally.

Meanwhile, in a large saucepan, bring 4 quarts of water to a boil over medium-high heat. Place the pasta in the boiling water, stir, and return to a boil. Cook until al dente, 10 to 12 minutes, stirring occasionally. Drain in a colander.

Transfer the pasta to warm serving plates. Spoon the cabbage sauce over the top and serve immediately.

Makes 4 servings

Per Serving:
309 Calories; 7g Protein; 12g Fat; 46g Carbohydrates; 22mg Cholesterol; 849mg Sodium; 7g Fiber.

Somen Noodles with Japanese Greens (Mizuna)

For this quick-and-light stir-fry, tender somen noodles are blended with strips of vegetables and Japanese mizuna, a feathery green with a mild mustardlike flavor.

8 ounces somen noodles
1 tablespoon canola oil
1 medium yellow onion, cut into thin slivers
1 red bell pepper, seeded and cut into thin strips
4 ounces extra-firm tofu, cut into matchsticks
1 medium bunch mizuna, trimmed and coarsely chopped (see Helpful Hint)
¼ cup low-sodium soy sauce
1 tablespoon dark brown sugar
½ teaspoon freshly ground black pepper

In a large saucepan, bring 3 quarts of water to a boil over medium-high heat. Place the noodles in the boiling water, stir, and return to a boil. Cook until al dente, 4 to 5 minutes, stirring occasionally. Drain in a colander.

Meanwhile, in a large skillet or wok, heat the oil over medium-high heat. Add the onion and bell pepper and cook, stirring, for about 5 minutes. Stir in the tofu, mizuna, soy sauce, brown sugar, and pepper and bring to a simmer. Cook, stirring, until the greens are wilted, about 4 minutes. Reduce the heat to low and gently fold in the somen noodles.

Transfer the noodle mixture to warm serving plates and serve immediately.

Makes 4 servings

Helpful Hint

Mizuna can be found in Asian markets, natural food stores, and well-stocked supermarkets. If mizuna is not available, try frisé, a French green with a similar texture and flavor.

Per Serving:
318 Calories; 13g Protein; 5g Fat; 55g Carbohydrates; 0 Cholesterol; 1,719mg Sodium; 6g Fiber.

105

Spinach Linguine with a Trio of Roasted Peppers

Bell peppers add a splash of color to this simple pasta dish. The noodles are coated with an herbed balsamic dressing. Whole wheat linguine or quinoa spaghetti can also be used (but remember to adjust the cooking time).

1 yellow pepper, cored and
  seeded
1 red bell pepper, cored and
  seeded
1 green bell pepper, cored and
  seeded
2 tablespoons balsamic vinegar
1 to 2 tablespoons olive oil or
  canola oil
2 cloves garlic, minced
1 teaspoon dried oregano
½ teaspoon dried basil
½ teaspoon freshly ground
  black pepper
½ teaspoon salt
12 ounces spinach linguine
2 ounces feta cheese, crumbled
  (optional)

Preheat the broiler.

Place the peppers on a baking pan. Place the pan beneath the broiler and broil until the skins are nearly charred and flaky, 6 to 8 minutes per side. Turn the peppers after 5 minutes. Remove the peppers from the heat and let cool slightly. With a butter knife, scrape off any charred or flaky spots. Cut the flesh into thin strips. Alternatively, use one 12-ounce jar of roasted bell peppers.

In a medium mixing bowl, whisk together the vinegar, oil, garlic, oregano, basil, pepper, and salt. Add the peppers and toss. Set aside for 5 minutes.

Meanwhile, in a large saucepan, bring 4 quarts of water to a boil over medium-high heat. Place the pasta in the boiling water, stir, and return to a boil. Cook until al dente, 9 to 11 minutes, stirring occasionally. Drain in a colander.

Combine the pasta with marinated peppers and feta (if desired). Toss again and serve immediately.

Per Serving:
325 Calories; 11g Protein; 8g Fat; 55g Carbohydrates; 95mg Cholesterol; 327mg Sodium; 3g Fiber.

Makes 4 servings

Spaghetti with Tempeh-Mushroom Tomato Sauce

*Tempeh gives this rustic red sauce a faux-meat texture and earthy flavor.
If tempeh is unavailable, try seitan or tofu.*

1 tablespoon canola oil
8 ounces button mushrooms,
   sliced
2 cloves garlic, minced
4 ounces tempeh, diced
One 28-ounce can tomato puree
2 teaspoons dried parsley
1 teaspoon dried basil
½ teaspoon freshly ground
   black pepper
½ teaspoon salt
12 ounces spaghetti
¼ cup shredded provolone
   cheese (optional)

In a large skillet, heat the oil over medium heat. Add the mushrooms and garlic and cook, stirring, for about 5 minutes. Stir in the tempeh and cook, stirring, for about 3 minutes more.

Stir in the tomato puree, parsley, basil, pepper, and salt and bring to a simmer. Cook for 15 to 20 minutes over medium-low heat, stirring occasionally.

Meanwhile, in a large saucepan, bring 4 quarts of water to a boil over medium-high heat. Place the spaghetti in the boiling water, stir, and return to a boil. Cook until al dente, 8 to 10 minutes, stirring occasionally. Drain in a colander.

Transfer the spaghetti to warm serving plates and ladle the sauce over the top. If desired, sprinkle with shredded cheese.

Makes 6 servings

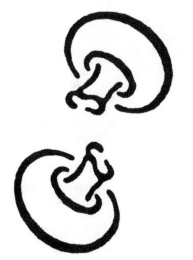

Per Serving:
385 Calories; 16g Protein; 5g Fat;
71g Carbohydrates; 0 Cholesterol;
725mg Sodium; 8g Fiber.

Lo Mein and Vegetable Stir-Fry with Tempeh

For this ultra-satisfying stir-fry, soft ribbonlike lo mein noodles
are juxtaposed with chewy tempeh, crunchy broccoli, and woodsy
mushrooms. A smidgen of peanut butter thickens the sauce while
adding a hint of nuttiness.

8 ounces wide lo mein noodles
1 tablespoon peanut oil
1 red bell pepper, seeded and
  cut into thin strips
4 ounces button mushrooms,
  sliced
2 ounces shiitake mushrooms,
  sliced
2 cloves garlic, minced
10 to 12 broccoli florets
4 ounces tempeh, diced
½ cup vegetable broth
¼ cup low-sodium soy sauce
1 tablespoon rice vinegar
1 tablespoon sesame oil
1 to 2 teaspoons chili-garlic
  paste
1 tablespoon peanut butter

In a large saucepan, bring 3 quarts of water to a boil over medium-high heat. Place the noodles in the boiling water, stir, and return to a boil. Cook until al dente, 4 to 5 minutes, stirring occasionally. Drain the noodles in a colander.

Meanwhile, in a large skillet or wok heat the oil over medium-high heat. Add the bell pepper, mushrooms, and garlic and cook, stirring, for about 5 minutes.

Stir in the broccoli and tempeh and stir-fry for 3 to 4 minutes more. Stir in the vegetable broth, soy sauce, vinegar, sesame oil, and chili-garlic paste (if desired) and bring to a simmer. Cook, stirring, about 4 minutes. Reduce the heat to low and blend in the peanut butter. Fold in the lo mein noodles.

Transfer the noodles mixture to warm serving plates and serve at once.

Makes 4 servings

Per Serving:
186 Calories; 8g Protein; 7g Fat; 22g Carbohydrates; 0 Cholesterol; 412mg Sodium; 3g Fiber.

Gourmet Ravioli with No-Cook Roasted Pepper Sauce

This dish was inspired by a classic Provençal sauce called rouille. The flavorful, no-cook sauce is made with leftover bread (it's economical!), roasted sweet peppers, and a touch of hot pepper. Ravioli revels in the sweet, smoky flavor of roasted red peppers.

4 thick slices of French or Italian bread, crusts removed

1½ cups diced roasted sweet peppers (one 12-ounce jar, drained)

1 to 2 tablespoons olive oil or canola oil

2 cloves garlic, minced

¼ teaspoon cayenne pepper

¼ teaspoon salt

1 pound pumpkin ravioli or cheese ravioli

¼ cup chopped fresh parsley

In a medium mixing bowl, soak the bread in warm water for about 5 seconds. Place the bread in a colander, drain, and gently squeeze out the excess water like a sponge.

Transfer the mass of bread to a blender or food processor fitted with a steel blade. Add the peppers, oil, garlic, cayenne, and salt. Process the mixture until smooth, about 5 seconds. Transfer the sauce to a bowl and set aside at room temperature.

Meanwhile, in a large saucepan, bring 4 quarts of water to a boil over medium-high heat. Place the ravioli in the boiling water, stir, and return to a boil. Cook until al dente, 12 to 15 minutes, stirring occasionally. Drain in a colander.

Place the ravioli on warm serving plates. Ladle the sauce over the top and sprinkle with parsley.

Makes 4 servings

VARIATION

If you prefer the sauce to be hot, heat the sauce in a saucepan over medium heat.

Per Serving:
364 Calories; 16g Protein; 10g Fat; 30g Carbohydrates; 0 Cholesterol; 551mg Sodium; 1g Fiber.

Macaroni Posole Stew

This New Mexican hot-pot of vegetables, stewed tomatoes, chili powder, and posole illustrates the versatility of the humble macaroni. Posole, also called hominy, is a chewy, puffed-up corn kernel that has been dried, rehydrated, and cooked (like dried beans).

1 cup elbow macaroni
2 teaspoons canola oil
1 medium yellow onion, diced
1 green bell pepper, seeded and
   diced
1 stalk celery, diced
1 large carrot, diced
3 to 4 cloves garlic, minced
One 28-ounce can stewed
   tomatoes, undrained
One 15-ounce can posole,
   drained (see Helpful Hint)
1 tablespoon chili powder
2 teaspoons dried oregano
½ teaspoon freshly ground
   black pepper
½ teaspoon salt

In a medium saucepan, bring 3 quarts of water to a boil over medium-high heat. Place the macaroni in the boiling water, stir, and return to a boil. Cook until al dente, about 6 minutes, stirring occasionally. Drain in a colander.

Meanwhile, in a large saucepan, heat the oil over medium-high heat. Add the onion, bell pepper, celery, carrot, and garlic and cook, stirring, for 7 minutes. Stir in the stewed tomatoes and all remaining ingredients and bring to a simmer. Cook over medium-low heat for 15 minutes, stirring occasionally. (Cut the stewed tomatoes into small pieces as you stir.)

Fold in the cooked macaroni and remove from the heat. Let stand for about 5 minutes before serving.

Ladle into bowls and serve with warm bread or flour tortillas.

Makes 6 servings

VARIATION

For spicier stew, add 1 jalapeño (seeded and minced) with the vegetables and 1 teaspoon ground cumin with the spices.

Helpful Hint

Canned posole can be found in well-stocked supermarkets—either in the canned vegetable aisle or near the canned beans.

Per Serving:
196 Calories; 5g Protein; 2g Fat; 38g Carbohydrates; 0 Cholesterol; 636mg Sodium; 5g Fiber.

Chinese Mushroom Soup

1 tablespoon peanut or
   vegetable oil
4 ounces assorted sliced exotic
   mushrooms
2 cloves garlic, minced
1 teaspoon minced fresh
   gingerroot
Two 14½-ounce cans vegetable
   broth
1½ cups water
2 tablespoons white miso
½ teaspoon hot chili oil
1½ cups (3 ounces) thin egg
   noodles
¼ cup thinly sliced scallions
1 teaspoon sesame oil

Heat the oil in a large saucepan
over medium heat. Add the
mushrooms, garlic, and ginger,
and cook, stirring, 5 minutes.

Add the broth, water, miso,
and chili oil; bring to a simmer.
Stir the noodles into the soup.
Return to a simmer and cook,
uncovered, until the noodles are
tender, 5 to 6 minutes.

Remove from the heat; stir in
scallions and sesame oil.

Makes 4 servings

Per Serving:
151 Calories; 5g Protein; 7g Fat; 19g
Carbohydrates; 14mg Cholesterol;
1,175mg Sodium; 2g Fiber.

Balsamic Roasted Vegetables with Gemelli

Nothing brings out the sweetness of vegetables like roasting. In this dish, use gemelli pasta, short twists of spaghetti that cook up quickly.

1 small red onion, cut into thin wedges

1 red bell pepper, cut into 1-inch chunks

1 yellow bell pepper, cut into 1-inch chunks

2 tablespoons garlic-infused olive oil

6 ounces garlic and basil or whole wheat gemelli

1 small zucchini, cut into ¼-inch slices

1 small yellow squash, cut into ¼-inch slices

1½ tablespoons balsamic vinegar

¼ teaspoon salt, or to taste

¼ teaspoon freshly ground black pepper

¼ cup basil leaves, cut chiffonade-style (see Helpful Hint, page 3)

Preheat oven to 475°F.

Combine the onion wedges and bell pepper chunks in a shallow metal roasting pan, jelly roll pan, or bottom of broiler pan. (Do not use a glass dish or vegetables will not brown.) Drizzle with 1 tablespoon of the oil; toss to lightly coat the vegetables with oil. Roast 10 minutes.

Meanwhile, in a medium saucepan, bring 3 quarts of water to a boil over medium-high heat. Place the pasta in the boiling water, stir, and return to a boil. Cook until al dente, 8 to 10 minutes, stirring occasionally.

After vegetables have roasted 10 minutes, add zucchini and yellow squash to pan; toss vegetables and continue roasting until the vegetables are golden brown on the edges and crisp-tender, about 10 minutes more. Remove from the oven.

Drizzle vinegar over the roasted vegetables; sprinkle with salt and pepper and toss.

Drain the pasta; toss with remaining 1 tablespoon of the oil. Add the roasted vegetables and basil to the pasta. Toss well; serve warm or at room temperature.

Per Serving:
149 Calories; 3g Protein; 7g Fat; 19g Carbohydrates; 0 Cholesterol; 154mg Sodium; 2g Fiber.

Makes 4 servings

French-Style Frittata

This hearty, colorful omelet sports a mustard tang.

Nonstick cooking spray
½ cup thinly sliced yellow or
    other sweet onion
1 cup cut fresh thin asparagus
    or French green beans
    (1-inch pieces)
5 large egg whites
1 large egg yolk
¼ cup evaporated skim milk or
    soy milk
1 tablespoon Dijon mustard
⅛ teaspoon freshly ground
    black pepper
1 cup cooked ditalini or bow tie
    pasta
⅓ cup rinsed, drained, and
    chopped, bottled roasted
    red peppers
⅓ cup diced Brie cheese
    (optional)

Preheat oven to 450°F.

Coat a heavy 10-inch, oven-proof, nonstick skillet with sloped sides with cooking spray. Add the onion and asparagus and cook, stirring, over medium heat until crisp-tender, 5 to 6 minutes.

In a medium bowl, combine the egg whites, egg yolk, milk, mustard, and pepper; beat with a fork until well blended. Stir in the pasta, red peppers, and, if desired, cheese.

Pour into the skillet over the asparagus mixture. Mix well, and spread evenly in the skillet. Reduce the heat to medium-low and cook until the eggs are set at the edges (center will be wet), about 5 minutes.

Place the skillet in the oven, and bake until center of frittata is set, 6 to 7 minutes.

Makes 4 servings

Per Serving:
115 Calories; 10g Protein; 2g Fat;
14g Carbohydrates; 54mg Cholesterol; 119mg Sodium; 2g Fiber.

Mostacciolini with Squash, Leeks, and Asiago

*The sweet flavor of fresh nutmeg is perfect in this
delicious fall squash dish.*

**8 ounces mostacciolini, baby
ziti, or penne**
1 small butternut squash
2 tablespoons butter
**2 medium leeks, white and
light green parts, thinly
sliced (1½ cups)**
¾ cup vegetable broth
**⅛ teaspoon freshly grated
nutmeg**
¼ cup grated Asiago cheese

In a large saucepan, bring 3 quarts of water to a boil over medium-high heat. Place the pasta in the boiling water, stir, and return to a boil. Cook until al dente, 8 to 10 minutes, stirring occasionally.

Meanwhile, peel the squash with a vegetable peeler. Cut the squash crosswise into ½-inch slices; discard the seeds. Cut the slices into ½-inch chunks (you need 2½ cups squash). Save any remaining squash for another use.

Melt the butter in a large skillet over medium-high heat. Add the squash and leeks, and cook, stirring, 2 minutes. Add the broth; cover and simmer until the squash is tender, 10 to 12 minutes.

Drain the pasta, and toss with the squash mixture. Sprinkle with nutmeg, then cheese.

Makes 4 servings

Per Serving:
314 Calories; 9g Protein; 9g Fat;
52g Carbohydrates; 21mg Cholesterol; 312mg Sodium; 3g Fiber.

Tomato Penne with Basil-Caper Sauce

**8 ounces sun-dried tomato
penne or tomato-basil fusilli
4 cups broccoli florets
¼ cup chopped fresh basil or
flat-leaf parsley
2 tablespoons garlic-infused
olive oil, or extra-virgin
olive oil plus 2 teaspoons
minced fresh garlic
1 tablespoon fresh lemon juice
1 tablespoon drained capers
1 teaspoon finely shredded
lemon peel
¼ teaspoon salt, or to taste
¼ teaspoon freshly ground
black pepper
½ cup (2 ounces) grated
Pecorino-Romano cheese
(optional)**

In a large saucepan, bring 3 quarts of water to a boil over medium-high heat. Place the pasta in the boiling water, stir, and return to a boil. Cook until al dente, 8 to 10 minutes, stirring occasionally, adding broccoli to water during last 3 minutes of cooking time.

Meanwhile, in a large bowl, combine basil or parsley, oil, lemon juice, capers, lemon peel, salt, and pepper; mix well. Drain pasta and broccoli, and add to basil mixture, tossing well. Sprinkle with cheese, if desired.

Makes 4 servings

Per Serving:
201 Calories; 7g Protein; 8g Fat; 29g Carbohydrates; 0 Cholesterol; 249mg Sodium; 4g Fiber.

Portabellos with Spinach and Noodles

Portabello mushrooms, rich in flavor and meaty texture, provide a creative oomph to this Asian-inspired noodle dish.

10 ounces chuka soba (Chinese or Japanese curly noodles or ramen) or 8 ounces vermicelli
4 large portabello mushrooms (about 1½ pounds)
3 tablespoons tamari or soy sauce
1 tablespoon rice vinegar
2 teaspoons chili-garlic paste
4 cloves garlic, minced
1½ tablespoons dark or "toasted" sesame oil
One 10-ounce package spinach leaves, stems discarded (8 cups packed)

In a large saucepan, bring 3 quarts of water to a boil over medium-high heat. Place the pasta in the boiling water, stir, and return to a boil. Cook until al dente, 8 to 10 minutes, stirring occasionally. Drain well in a colander. Meanwhile, preheat broiler.

Trim the mushroom stems to 1 inch. Place the mushrooms stem-side down on the rack of a broiler pan.

In a small bowl, combine 2 tablespoons of the tamari or soy sauce, vinegar, chili-garlic paste, and garlic; brush half of the mixture over the mushroom caps. Broil the mushrooms 4 to 5 inches from the heat source for 5 minutes. Turn and spoon the remaining tamari mixture into the mushroom caps. Continue broiling until the mushrooms are tender, 4 to 5 minutes. Transfer the mushrooms to a chopping board, reserving any juices in broiler pan.

Add the sesame oil and spinach to the pasta cooking pot. Cover and cook over medium heat until the spinach wilts, about 1 minute. Add the drained noodles and the remaining 1 tablespoon tamari to the pot; toss well and heat through.

Cut mushroom caps into ½-inch slices, and serve atop the noodle mixture. Drizzle any remaining mushroom juices from the broiler pan over the mushrooms and noodles.

Makes 4 to 6 servings

Per Serving:
412 Calories; 19g Protein; 7g Fat; 65g Carbohydrates; 0 Cholesterol; 1,228mg Sodium; 9g Fiber.

Two-Bean Jalapeño Chili Mac

*Serve this delightful chili mac with warm corn tortillas
or baked tortilla chips.*

6 ounces corn, whole wheat or
   regular medium pasta, such
   as shells or elbows
1 tablespoon vegetable oil
1 large onion, chopped
2 cups diced red, yellow and
   green bell peppers
4 cloves garlic, minced
One 15- or 16-ounce can meatless chili beans in spicy
   sauce, undrained
One 15- or 16-ounce can pinto or
   black beans, rinsed and
   drained
½ cup vegetable broth or water
2 teaspoons chili powder
2 teaspoons bottled minced
   jalapeño peppers or
   1 jalapeño pepper, minced
1 teaspoon ground cumin
Optional toppings: shredded
   Monterey Jack cheese with
   jalapeño peppers, sour
   cream, salsa, chopped
   cilantro, diced avocado,
   chopped tomato

In a large saucepan, bring 3 quarts of water to a boil over medium-high heat. Place the pasta in the boiling water, stir, and return to a boil. Cook until al dente, 8 to 10 minutes, stirring occasionally.

Meanwhile, heat the oil in a large saucepan over medium-high heat. Add the onion and cook, stirring, 3 minutes. Add the bell peppers and garlic and cook, stirring, 2 minutes. Add the beans, broth or water, chili powder, jalapeño peppers, and cumin. Bring to a boil, reduce heat to low, and simmer until the vegetables are tender, about 10 minutes.

Drain the pasta and add it to the saucepan with the bean mixture. Mix well and simmer 2 minutes. Ladle into shallow bowls; serve with optional toppings, if desired.

The chili mac can be made up to 4 days in advance. Add a little broth or water if it becomes too thick.

Makes 4 servings

Per Serving:
384 Calories; 15g Protein; 6g Fat;
75g Carbohydrates; 0.4mg Cholesterol; 1,082mg Sodium; 15g Fiber.

Hoppin' John Pasta Supper

Hoppin' John is a traditional Southern New Year's Day dish of black-eyed peas seasoned with pork and served with rice. This meatless version is served over pasta.

8 ounces medium whole wheat, corn, or quinoa pasta, such as shells or penne
2 tablespoons vegetable oil
1 large onion, chopped (about 1½ cups)
1 green bell pepper, chopped (about 1 cup)
4 cloves garlic, minced
Two 14½-ounce cans Cajun-style stewed tomatoes, undrained
One 16-ounce can black-eyed peas, rinsed and drained
½ teaspoon hot pepper sauce, or to taste
¼ teaspoon salt, or to taste
¼ cup chopped fresh parsley

In a large saucepan, bring 3 quarts of water to a boil over medium-high heat. Place the pasta in the boiling water, stir, and return to a boil. Cook until al dente, 8 to 10 minutes, stirring occasionally.

Meanwhile, heat the oil in a large saucepan over medium-high heat. Add the onion, and cook, stirring, 5 minutes. Add the bell pepper and garlic, and sauté 3 minutes more.

Add the tomatoes, peas, hot pepper sauce, and salt. Cover and bring to a boil. Then immediately reduce the heat to low, cover, and simmer until the vegetables are crisp-tender, 10 to 12 minutes.

Drain the pasta in a colander, and transfer to 4 shallow bowls. Top with the black-eyed peas mixture, and sprinkle with parsley.

Makes 5 servings

Per Serving:
314 Calories; 13g Protein; 6g Fat; 58g Carbohydrates; 0 Cholesterol; 796mg Sodium; 10g Fiber.

Tuscan Pasta Primavera

6 ounces medium pasta or
garlic-flavored pasta, such
as bow ties, penne, or
mostaccioli
2 tablespoons olive oil
4 cloves garlic, minced
One 16-ounce package frozen
mixed vegetables (such as
broccoli, green beans, pearl
onions, and red bell pep-
pers), thawed
One 14½-ounce can seasoned
diced tomatoes, undrained
1 tablespoon chopped fresh
rosemary or 1 teaspoon
dried rosemary, crushed
One 16- or 19-ounce can
cannellini beans, rinsed and
drained
1 tablespoon balsamic vinegar
Freshly ground black pepper

In a large saucepan, bring 3 quarts
of water to a boil over medium-
high heat. Place the pasta in the
boiling water, stir, and return
to a boil. Cook until al dente, 8 to
10 minutes, stirring occasionally.

Meanwhile, heat the oil in a
large deep skillet over medium
heat. Add the garlic, and cook,
stirring, 2 minutes. Add the
thawed vegetables, tomatoes, and
rosemary, and bring to a simmer.
Reduce the heat to low and
simmer, uncovered, 5 minutes. Stir
in the beans, and heat through.

Drain the pasta in a colander,
and add it to the bean mixture.
Add the vinegar; toss well and
heat through. Serve with pepper.

Makes 4 servings

Per Serving:
363 Calories; 14g Protein; 10g Fat;
63g Carbohydrates; 0 Cholesterol;
955mg Sodium; 14g Fiber.

Red Bell Pepper Fettuccine with Braised Endive

Endive braised in broth and wine makes for an elegant dish.

8 ounces red bell pepper or whole wheat fettuccine or linguine
1 tablespoon olive oil
4 cloves garlic, minced
1 cup plus 3 tablespoons vegetable broth
⅓ cup white wine such as Rhine or Riesling
½ teaspoon sugar
4 medium heads endive (about 12 ounces), halved lengthwise, then cut crosswise into 1-inch pieces
1 medium yellow, orange, or red bell pepper, cut into short, thin strips
2½ teaspoons cornstarch
⅓ cup grated Asiago cheese
Freshly ground black pepper

In a large saucepan, bring 3 quarts of water to a boil over medium-high heat. Place the pasta in the boiling water, stir, and return to a boil. Cook until al dente, 5 to 7 minutes, stirring occasionally.

Meanwhile, heat the oil in a large deep skillet over medium heat. Add the garlic and cook, stirring, 1 minute. Stir in 1 cup of the broth, the wine, and sugar, and bring to a boil. Add the endive and bell pepper. Reduce the heat to low, cover, and simmer until the vegetables are crisp-tender, about 7 minutes.

In a cup or a small bowl, stir together the cornstarch and remaining 3 tablespoons broth until smooth. Stir into the endive mixture. Simmer, uncovered, stirring frequently, until the sauce thickens, about 2 minutes.

Drain the pasta in a colander, and transfer to four serving plates. Spoon endive mixture over pasta; sprinkle with cheese and serve with pepper.

Makes 4 servings

Per Serving:
315 Calories; 11g Protein; 7g Fat; 49g Carbohydrates; 7mg Cholesterol; 332mg Sodium; 5g Fiber.

Tomato Penne with Potatoes and Bitter Greens

1¼ **pounds medium red potatoes, cut into slices no
thicker than ¼ inch**
2 **tablespoons garlic-infused
olive oil**
8 **ounces sun-dried tomato
penne or mostaccioli**
1 **tablespoon butter**
1 **large yellow or other sweet
onion, thinly sliced, separated into rings**
¾ **teaspoon salt, or to taste**
¼ **teaspoon freshly ground
black pepper**
1 ½ **tablespoons fresh lemon
juice or white balsamic
vinegar**
2 ½ **cups (3 ounces) packed
arugula or mesclun (see
Helpful Hint)**
**Freshly grated Parmesan
cheese (optional)**

Preheat oven to 450°F.

Toss potato slices with 1 tablespoon of the oil; arrange in a
single layer in a shallow roasting
pan, jelly roll pan, or broiler pan
without the rack. Roast until
golden brown, about 15 to 20
minutes.

Meanwhile, in a large saucepan,
bring 3 quarts of water to a boil
over medium-high heat. Place the
pasta in the boiling water, stir,
and return to a boil. Cook until al
dente, 8 to 10 minutes, stirring
occasionally.

Melt the butter in a large skillet
over medium-high heat. Add the
onion rings and cook, stirring,
until transparent, about 3 minutes.
Reduce the heat to medium, and
cook, stirring, until golden brown
and tender, 8 to 10 minutes more.

Remove the potatoes from the
oven, add to the skillet, and
sprinkle with ½ teaspoon salt and
pepper.

Drain the pasta in a colander,
and return it to the pot. Add the
remaining 1 tablespoon oil, lemon
juice, and remaining ¼ teaspoon
salt; toss. Add the arugula or
mesclun and toss well. Add the
potatoes and onions and toss
gently.

Serve warm or at room temperature with cheese, if desired.

Makes 5 servings

Helpful Hint

*Mesclun is a mixture of young salad
greens sold in the produce section of
most supermarkets.*

Per Serving:
313 Calories; 7g Protein; 9g Fat;
53g Carbohydrates; 7mg Cholesterol; 383mg Sodium; 5g Fiber.

121

Garden Ravioli with Brussels Sprouts

2 cups (9 ounces) halved fresh Brussels sprouts or one 9-ounce package frozen Brussels sprouts, thawed
One 9-ounce package refrigerated vegetable and cheese ravioli
1 tablespoon butter
½ cup chopped shallots, yellow or other sweet onion, or thinly sliced leek
4 cloves garlic, minced
1 teaspoon all-purpose flour
1 cup evaporated skim milk or soy milk
1 tablespoon Dijon mustard with peppercorns or regular Dijon mustard
1 tablespoon chopped fresh rosemary, tarragon, or thyme or ¼ cup chopped chives or garlic chives
Freshly ground black pepper

Bring a large pot of water to a rolling boil. Add the Brussels sprouts, return to a boil, and boil gently 2 minutes. Add the ravioli to the pot with the Brussels sprouts, return to a boil and boil gently until the sprouts and ravioli are tender, 4 to 5 minutes.

Meanwhile, melt the butter in a medium saucepan over medium heat. Add the shallots, and cook, stirring, 5 minutes. Add the garlic, and cook, stirring, 1 minute more. Add the flour, and cook, stirring, 1 minute.

Add the milk, and bring to a simmer, stirring frequently. Reduce the heat to low and simmer until sauce thickens slightly, about 2 minutes. Remove from the heat, and stir in the mustard and rosemary. Drain the sprouts and ravioli, add to the sauce, and toss to combine. Serve with pepper.

Makes 3 servings

Per Serving:
309 Calories; 18g Protein; 8g Fat; 45g Carbohydrates; 49mg Cholesterol; 373mg Sodium; 6g Fiber.

Asian Noodle Stir-Fry

8 ounces brown rice vermicelli or whole wheat spaghetti
1 tablespoon peanut or vegetable oil
8 ounces shiitake mushrooms, stems discarded, caps sliced
1 cup (2 ounces) julienned carrots
One 8¾-ounce can or 7-ounce jar baby corn on the cob, drained and rinsed
1 cup fresh bean sprouts or ½ cup drained canned sliced water chestnuts
¼ cup water
1 teaspoon cornstarch
¼ cup teriyaki sauce
¼ cup thinly sliced scallions

In a large saucepan, bring 3 quarts of water to a boil over medium-high heat. Place the pasta in the boiling water, stir, and return to a boil. Cook until al dente, about 2 minutes for vermicelli and 8 to 10 minutes for spaghetti, stirring occasionally.

Meanwhile, heat the oil in a large nonstick skillet or wok over medium-high heat. Add the mushrooms and carrots, and cook, stirring, 3 minutes. Add the corn and bean sprouts or water chestnuts, and cook, stirring, 1 minute more.

In a cup, stir together the water and cornstarch until smooth; add it to the skillet with the teriyaki sauce. Cook, stirring, until the sauce thickens, about 2 minutes.

Drain the noodles in a colander and place on 4 serving plates. Top with stir-fry and sprinkle with scallions.

Makes 4 servings

Per Serving:
519 Calories; 12g Protein; 6g Fat; 100g Carbohydrates; 0 Cholesterol; 354mg Sodium; 5g Fiber.

Tricolor Fusilli with Fresh Tomatoes and Goat Cheese

8 ounces tricolored or regular fusilli

1 pound (2 large or 3 medium) very ripe tomatoes, seeded and chopped

½ cup vegetable broth

4 cloves garlic, minced

1 tablespoon chopped fresh thyme or 1 teaspoon dried

2 teaspoons extra-virgin olive oil

2 teaspoons balsamic vinegar

½ teaspoon salt, or to taste

¼ teaspoon freshly ground black pepper

4 ounces herbed goat cheese, crumbled

In a large saucepan, bring 3 quarts of water to a boil over medium-high heat. Place the pasta in the boiling water, stir, and return to a boil. Cook until al dente, 6 to 8 minutes, stirring occasionally.

Meanwhile, combine all of the remaining ingredients except the goat cheese in a medium to large bowl; set aside.

Drain the pasta in a colander and return it to the pot. Add the tomato mixture and cook over medium heat until hot, tossing well, about 2 minutes.

Add the goat cheese and cook until it melts and the sauce thickens, tossing constantly. Serve with additional freshly ground black pepper, if desired.

Makes 4 servings

Per Serving:
336 Calories; 13g Protein; 10g Fat; 49g Carbohydrates; 13mg Cholesterol; 534mg Sodium; 4g Fiber.

Pappardelle with Florentine Sauce

Pappardelle are wide noodles with ruffled sides; tagliatelle is what northern Italians call fettuccine. Use either in this dish.

8 ounces pappardelle or tagliatelle
2 tablespoons olive oil
4 cloves garlic, minced
2 tablespoons all-purpose flour
One 14¼-ounce can diced seasoned tomatoes, undrained
1 cup vegetable broth
½ teaspoon red pepper flakes
One 10-ounce package frozen chopped spinach, thawed and squeezed dry
¼ cup chopped fresh basil
¼ cup grated Asiago cheese (optional)

In a large saucepan, bring 3 quarts of water to a boil over medium-high heat. Place the pasta in the boiling water, stir, and return to a boil. Cook until al dente, 8 to 10 minutes, stirring occasionally.

Meanwhile, heat the oil in a medium saucepan over medium heat. Add the garlic and cook, stirring, 1 minute. Add the flour and cook 1 minute more. Add the tomatoes, broth, and pepper flakes; bring to a boil, stirring occasionally.

Stir in the spinach, and return to a boil. Remove from the heat and stir in the basil.

Drain the pasta and return it to the pot. Add the sauce and toss to coat. Sprinkle with cheese, if desired.

Makes 4 servings

Per Serving:
293 Calories; 9g Protein; 10g Fat; 45g Carbohydrates; 0 Cholesterol; 845mg Sodium; 5g Fiber.

Stir-Fried Spicy Eggplant and Noodles

6 ounces medium egg noodles
1½ tablespoons peanut or
**   vegetable oil**
1 small eggplant (about
**   1 pound) peeled, cut into**
**   ¾-inch chunks**
4 cloves garlic, minced
¾ cup vegetable broth
¼ cup ketchup
2 tablespoons tamari or soy
**   sauce**
1 tablespoon chili-garlic paste
1½ teaspoons dark or "toasted"
**   sesame oil**
3 cups sliced napa or Chinese
**   cabbage**

In a large saucepan, bring 3 quarts of water to a boil over medium-high heat. Place the pasta in the boiling water, stir, and return to a boil. Cook until al dente, 8 to 10 minutes, stirring occasionally.

Meanwhile, heat the oil in a large, deep, nonstick skillet over medium-high heat until hot. Add the eggplant and cook, stirring, 2 minutes. Add the garlic and cook, stirring, 2 minutes more.

Add the broth, ketchup, tamari or soy sauce, chili-garlic paste, and sesame oil. Reduce the heat and simmer, uncovered, until the sauce thickens and the eggplant is tender, about 3 minutes. Stir in the cabbage and cook, stirring, 1 minute.

Drain the noodles in a colander and add them to the eggplant mixture; toss well.

Makes 4 servings

Per Serving:
287 Calories; 10g Protein; 9g Fat; 44g Carbohydrates; 40mg Cholesterol; 890mg Sodium; 5g Fiber.

Fusilli with Peas and Radicchio

8 ounces regular or tricolored fusilli
2 tablespoons butter
1 large yellow or other sweet onion, chopped
1 cup julienned carrots
1 tablespoon all-purpose flour
1 cup vegetable broth
2 tablespoons prepared honey mustard
1 cup frozen peas
1 cup packed sliced radicchio leaves
Freshly ground black pepper

In a large saucepan, bring 3 quarts of water to a boil over medium-high heat. Place the pasta in the boiling water, stir, and return to a boil. Cook until al dente, 6 to 8 minutes, stirring occasionally.

Meanwhile, melt the butter in a large, nonstick skillet over medium heat. Add the onion and carrots and cook, stirring, until the onion is golden brown, about 8 minutes. Sprinkle the onion with the flour and cook 1 minute.

Add the broth and mustard. Bring to a simmer and add the peas. Return to a simmer and stir in the radicchio. Remove from the heat.

Drain the pasta and add it to the skillet with the sauce. Toss well. Sprinkle with pepper to taste.

Makes 4 servings

Per Serving:
307 Calories; 9g Protein; 8g Fat; 51g Carbohydrates; 16mg Cholesterol; 422mg Sodium; 4g Fiber.

Vietnamese-Style Noodles

One 7-ounce package rice
  sticks or capellini,
  uncooked
2 cups sliced spinach leaves
1 cup shredded carrots
One 7.8-ounce jar marinated
  hearts of palm
2 serrano chili peppers, minced,
  or ¾ teaspoon red pepper
  flakes
¼ cup tamari or soy sauce
1 tablespoon brown sugar
3 cloves garlic, minced
½ cup chopped cilantro
3 tablespoons chopped fresh
  mint leaves

In a large saucepan, bring 3 quarts of water to a boil over medium-high heat. Place the pasta in the boiling water, stir, and return to a boil. Cook until al dente, 2 to 3 minutes, stirring occasionally.

Meanwhile, combine the spinach and carrots in a large bowl.

Drain the hearts of palm, reserving the marinade. Coarsely chop hearts of palm; add to the spinach and carrots and toss.

In a small bowl, combine the reserved marinade with all of the remaining ingredients except the cilantro and mint.

Drain the pasta in a colander and toss with the spinach mixture until the spinach wilts. Add the marinade mixture, cilantro, and mint and toss again. Serve warm or at room temperature.

Makes 4 servings

VARIATION

If marinated hearts of palm are not available, substitute ¾ cup coarsely chopped regular canned hearts of palm and add 2 tablespoons vegetable or peanut oil to replace the marinade.

Per Serving:
275 Calories; 5g Protein; 0.4g Fat;
65g Carbohydrates; 0 Cholesterol;
1,054mg Sodium; 3g Fiber.

Pasta Palermo

**8 ounces baby penne or
    mostacciolini**
½ cup golden or dark raisins
**4 cups packed torn spinach
    leaves (4 ounces)**
**2½ cups (1 recipe) Fresh
    No-Cook Tomato-Ricotta
    Sauce (page 183)**
**¼ cup pine nuts, toasted
    (optional; see Helpful Hint,
    page 71)**

In a large saucepan, bring 3 quarts of water to a boil over medium-high heat. Place the pasta in the boiling water, stir, and return to a boil. Cook until al dente, 8 to 10 minutes, stirring occasionally, adding the raisins to the pasta during the last 5 minutes of cooking. Add the spinach during the last minute of cooking.

Meanwhile, prepare Fresh No-Cook Tomato-Ricotta Sauce.

Drain the pasta, raisins, and spinach in a colander and toss with the sauce. Sprinkle with pine nuts, if desired.

Makes 4 servings

Per Serving:
382 Calories; 17g Protein; 10g Fat; 59g Carbohydrates; 10mg Cholesterol; 448mg Sodium; 6g Fiber.

Middle Eastern Tomato Stew

6 ounces cavatelli or galetti

One 15-ounce can chickpeas (garbanzo beans), rinsed and drained

One 14½-ounce can diced tomatoes with garlic and onion, undrained

1 cup vegetable broth

½ cup golden or dark raisins

½ teaspoon cardamom

½ teaspoon ground cumin

¼ teaspoon cinnamon

4 cups packed torn spinach leaves (4 ounces)

2 tablespoons chopped mint leaves

1 teaspoon finely shredded lemon peel

In a large saucepan, bring 3 quarts of water to a boil over medium-high heat. Place the pasta in the boiling water, stir, and return to a boil. Cook until al dente, 8 to 10 minutes, stirring occasionally.

Meanwhile, combine the chickpeas, tomatoes, broth, raisins, cardamom, cumin, and cinnamon in a large deep skillet. Bring to a boil, then immediately reduce heat to low. Simmer, uncovered, 5 minutes.

Stir in the spinach; simmer 1 minute.

Drain the pasta in a colander and add it to the chickpea mixture. Simmer 1 minute. Ladle into shallow bowls. In a cup or small bowl, combine the mint and lemon peel and sprinkle over the stew.

Makes 4 servings

Per Serving:
351 Calories; 13g Protein; 4g Fat; 70g Carbohydrates; 0 Cholesterol; 1,154mg Sodium; 9g Fiber.

Gnocchi en Brodo with Fava Beans

Serve this glorious Italian soup with crusty sourdough rolls.

Two 14½-ounce cans vegetable broth
¼ teaspoon red pepper flakes
16 ounces gnocchi
One 19-ounce can fava beans, rinsed and drained
1 cup diced tomato
⅓ cup basil leaves, cut chiffonade-style (see Helpful Hint, page 3)
1 tablespoon garlic- or roasted garlic-infused olive oil
½ cup freshly grated Romano or Asiago cheese (optional)

Combine the broth and pepper flakes in a large deep skillet. Bring to a boil over high heat. Add the gnocchi, and return to a boil.

Reduce the heat and simmer, uncovered, until gnocchi float to the surface, 3 to 4 minutes. Add the beans and tomato; simmer 3 minutes more. Add basil and oil. Ladle into shallow bowls; top with cheese, if desired.

Makes 4 servings

Per Serving:
361 Calories; 15g Protein; 13g Fat; 6g Carbohydrates; 22mg Cholesterol; 1,265mg Sodium; 8g Fiber.

Sonora-Style Pasta

Roasted garlic provides the slightly smoky flavor in this Southwest-inspired dish. If canned hominy is not available, substitute a can of black beans.

8 ounces rigatoni or
    mostaccioli
1 tablespoon vegetable oil
1 medium onion, chopped
1 red or yellow bell pepper,
    diced
4 cloves bottled, roasted garlic,
    minced
One 15-ounce can hominy or
    black beans, rinsed and
    drained
One 10-ounce can mild enchi-
    lada sauce
½ cup picante sauce or salsa
½ cup frozen whole kernel corn
½ teaspoon salt, or to taste
½ cup chopped cilantro
Sour cream (optional)

In a large saucepan, bring 3 quarts of water to a boil over medium-high heat. Place the pasta in the boiling water, stir, and return to a boil. Cook until al dente, 8 to 10 minutes, stirring occasionally.

Meanwhile, heat the oil in a large skillet over medium-high heat. Add the onion and cook, stirring, 5 minutes. Add the bell pepper and garlic and cook, stirring, 3 minutes more.

Add the hominy or black beans, enchilada sauce, picante sauce or salsa, corn, and salt; bring to a simmer. Reduce heat to low and simmer, uncovered, 5 minutes.

Drain the pasta, and toss it with the sauce and the cilantro. Serve with sour cream, if desired.

Makes 4 servings

Per Serving:
387 Calories; 13g Protein; 7g Fat;
71g Carbohydrates; 0 Cholesterol;
768mg Sodium; 6g Fiber.

Curried Almond Tofu and Vegetables

8 ounces regular or whole
    wheat spaghetti or linguine
2 teaspoons vegetable oil
4 cloves garlic, minced
1 teaspoon finely shredded
    fresh gingerroot
1 tablespoon all-purpose flour
One 14½-ounce can vegetable
    broth
1½ teaspoons curry powder
½ teaspoon salt, or to taste
¼ teaspoon cayenne pepper
    (omit if using hot Madras
    curry powder)
One 16-ounce package frozen
    vegetable mixture, such as
    broccoli, red bell peppers,
    and cauliflower
One 10½-ounce package low-
    fat, extra-firm tofu
½ cup finely diced Granny
    Smith apple
1 teaspoon dark or "toasted"
    sesame oil
3 tablespoons sliced almonds,
    toasted
Optional condiments: plain
    yogurt, mango chutney,
    toasted shredded coconut

In a large saucepan, bring 3 quarts of water to a boil over medium-high heat. Place the pasta in the boiling water, stir, and return to a boil. Cook until al dente, 8 to 10 minutes, stirring occasionally.

Meanwhile, heat the oil in a medium saucepan over medium heat. Add the garlic and ginger and cook, stirring, 2 minutes. Add the flour and cook, stirring, 1 minute. Add the broth, curry powder, salt, and cayenne pepper; bring to a boil, stirring frequently.

Add the vegetable mixture. Return to a boil over high heat, then immediately reduce heat to low. Simmer, uncovered, stirring occasionally, until the vegetables are tender and the sauce thickens, about 5 minutes.

Drain the tofu and cut it into ¾-inch cubes. Add the tofu to the vegetable mixture and stir in the apple and sesame oil.

Drain the pasta in a colander and add it to the tofu mixture; toss well. Sprinkle with almonds; serve with condiments, if desired.

Makes 5 servings

Per Serving:
283 Calories; 13g Protein; 7g Fat;
45g Carbohydrates; 0 Cholesterol;
657mg Sodium; 8g Fiber.

Straw and Hay Pasta with Creamy Sun-Dried Tomato Sauce

8 ounces spinach and egg fettuccine
2 cups cut fresh asparagus (1-inch pieces) or broccoli florets
1 tablespoon garlic- or roasted garlic-infused olive oil
1 tablespoon all-purpose flour
One 12-ounce can evaporated skim milk
3 tablespoons sun-dried tomato pesto (see Helpful Hint)
¼ teaspoon salt, or to taste
½ cup freshly grated Parmesan cheese (optional)
Freshly ground black pepper

In a large saucepan, bring 3 quarts of water to a boil over medium-high heat. Place the pasta in the boiling water, stir, and return to a boil. Cook until al dente, 8 to 10 minutes, stirring occasionally, adding the asparagus or broccoli to the pasta cooking water during the last 3 minutes of cooking.

Meanwhile, heat the oil in a large saucepan over medium heat. Add the flour and cook, stirring, 1 minute. Add the milk. Bring the mixture to a simmer, stirring occasionally. Stir in the pesto; simmer until the sauce thickens, about 3 minutes.

Drain the fettuccine and asparagus or broccoli in a colander; add to the sauce and toss well. Sprinkle with salt and cheese, if desired. Serve with pepper.

Makes 4 servings

Helpful Hint

Sun-dried tomato pesto is sold in most natural food stores and supermarkets.

Per Serving:
389 Calories; 18g Protein; 11g Fat; 54g Carbohydrates; 56mg Cholesterol; 383mg Sodium; 5g Fiber.

Five-Spice Udon Noodles

Five-spice powder is a Chinese seasoning mixture of Szechuan pepper, cinnamon, cloves, fennel seed, and star anise. Look for it in the Chinese food section or spice section of your supermarket.

8 ounces udon noodles or spaghetti

½ ounce dried wood ear mushrooms

½ cup boiling water

2 teaspoons chili oil or 2 teaspoons vegetable oil plus ½ teaspoon red pepper flakes

1 yellow or red bell pepper, chopped

4 cloves garlic, minced

1 teaspoon finely shredded fresh gingerroot

½ teaspoon five-spice powder

One 14½-ounce can vegetable broth

2 cups (6 ounces) halved fresh snow peas

One 15-ounce can straw mushrooms, drained

3 tablespoons tamari or soy sauce

1 tablespoon cornstarch

1 teaspoon dark or "toasted" sesame oil

In a large saucepan, boil 3 quarts of water over medium-high heat. Place the pasta in the boiling water, stir, and return to a boil. Cook until al dente, 8 to 10 minutes, stirring occasionally. Meanwhile, soak the dried mushrooms in the boiling water 15 minutes.

Heat the oil in a large, deep skillet over medium heat. Add the bell pepper, garlic, and ginger and cook, stirring, 4 minutes. Sprinkle the vegetables with the five-spice powder; cook, stirring, 1 minute more. Add the broth and snow peas; bring to a simmer.

Drain the mushrooms, reserving the soaking liquid. Add the mushrooms to the bell pepper mixture. Pour the reserved mushroom liquid into the skillet, being careful not to pour in any sediment in the bottom of the bowl. Stir in the straw mushrooms.

In a cup, stir together the tamari or soy sauce and the cornstarch until smooth. Stir the cornstarch mixture into the vegetable mixture and simmer until the sauce thickens and snow peas are crisp-tender, stirring frequently, 1 to 2 minutes. Stir in the sesame oil. Drain the noodles, add to the vegetable mixture and toss well.

Makes 4 servings

Per Serving:
339 Calories; 16g Protein; 6g Fat; 61g Carbohydrates; 0 Cholesterol; 1,890 mg Sodium; 5g Fiber.

Turkish Tahini Pasta

Tahini (sesame seed paste) gives this exotic pasta dish a delicious flavor, and turmeric adds a rich golden color.

8 ounces tagliatelle or
    fettuccine
1 pound baby carrots
1½ teaspoons chili oil, or
    1½ teaspoons vegetable
    oil and ¼ teaspoon red
    pepper flakes
1 medium onion, chopped
4 cloves garlic, minced
1 teaspoon all-purpose flour
One 14½-ounce can vegetable
    broth
⅓ cup golden or dark raisins
3 tablespoons tahini
    (sesame seed paste)
½ teaspoon turmeric
½ teaspoon salt, or to taste
½ cup chopped cilantro
Lemon wedges

In a large saucepan, bring 3 quarts of water to a boil over medium-high heat. Place the pasta in the boiling water, stir, and return to a boil. Cook until al dente, 8 to 10 minutes, stirring occasionally, adding the carrots to the pasta cooking water during the last 5 minutes of cooking.

Meanwhile, heat the oil in a large nonstick skillet over medium heat. Add the onion and cook, stirring, 5 minutes. Add the garlic and cook, stirring, 1 minute. Sprinkle the flour over the vegetables and cook, stirring, 1 minute more.

Add the broth and bring to a boil over high heat. Add the raisins, tahini, turmeric, and salt and return to a simmer. Simmer, uncovered, until the sauce thickens, stirring occasionally, about 5 minutes.

Drain the pasta and carrots in a colander; toss with the sauce and cilantro. Squeeze a little fresh lemon juice over the pasta just before serving.

Makes 4 servings

Per Serving:
311 Calories; 9g Protein; 6g Fat;
60g Carbohydrates; 0 Cholesterol;
782mg Sodium; 7g Fiber.

CHAPTER 2

Sides and Salads

Orzo Tabbouleh

It seems that everyone has eaten tabbouleh before, so it is fun to stray from the norm and improvise with this classic Middle Eastern wheat salad. For this rendition, orzo adds a welcome bit of sustenance to what ordinarily is a light dish.

1 cup bulgur
2 cups boiling water
1 cup orzo
4 scallions, trimmed and chopped
½ cup chopped fresh parsley
2 tablespoons chopped fresh mint (optional)
2 medium tomatoes, diced
1 medium cucumber, peeled and diced
Juice of 2 lemons
2 tablespoons olive oil
1 teaspoon freshly ground black pepper
1 teaspoon salt

Combine the bulgur and boiling water in a pan, cover, and let stand until the grains are tender, about 20 minutes. Drain off any excess liquid.

Meanwhile, in a medium saucepan, bring 2 quarts of water to a boil over medium-high heat. Place the orzo in the boiling water, stir, and return to a boil. Cook until al dente, 8 to 10 minutes, stirring occasionally. Drain the orzo in a colander and cool under cold running water.

In a mixing bowl, combine the remaining ingredients and toss thoroughly. Fold in the bulgur and cooked orzo. Refrigerate for 30 minutes to 1 hour before serving.

Makes 4 servings

VARIATIONS

Serve over a bed of leafy greens. If desired, offer warm pita bread on the side.

Per Serving:
328 Calories; 10g Protein; 8g Fat; 58g Carbohydrates; 0 Cholesterol; 600mg Sodium; 10g Fiber.

Mediterranean Orzo Salad

*Mint, oregano, and parsley—three favorite herbs of the Mediterranean
kitchen—lend an herbal fragrance to this light pasta salad.
The vinaigrette-style dressing is assertive without being overbearing.
Feta and black olives complete the picture.*

1 cup orzo
2 tablespoons olive oil
**2 tablespoons balsamic vinegar
or red wine vinegar**
1 tablespoon Dijon mustard
¼ cup chopped fresh parsley
**2 tablespoons chopped fresh
mint or 1 teaspoon dried**
2 teaspoons dried oregano
**½ teaspoon freshly ground
black pepper**
**10 to 12 yellow or red cherry
tomatoes, halved**
**4 scallions, trimmed and
chopped**
**1 cup cooked chickpeas,
drained**
**½ cup canned pitted black
olives, halved**
**2 ounces feta cheese, crumbled
(optional)**
2 cloves garlic, minced

In a large saucepan, bring 2 quarts
of water to a boil over medium-
high heat. Place the orzo in the
boiling water, stir, and return to a
boil. Cook until al dente, 7 to 8
minutes, stirring occasionally.
Drain the pasta in a colander and
cool under cold running water.

In a large mixing bowl, whisk
together the oil, vinegar, mustard,
parsley, mint, oregano, and
pepper. Stir in all of the remaining
ingredients.

Fold in the cooked orzo. Let
stand for 15 minutes to allow the
flavors to develop. Serve as a
warm salad, or refrigerate and
serve as a cold dish.

Makes 4 servings

VARIATIONS

*For a special twist, use a gourmet
olive such as kalamata, Sicilian, or
Niçoise instead of the canned olives.*

Per Serving:
149 Calories; 4g Protein; 6g Fat;
18g Carbohydrates; 0 Cholesterol;
74mg Sodium; 4g Fiber.

Orecchiette and Double Bean Salad

Just when you thought you'd seen every imaginable shape and size of pasta on the planet, along comes orecchiette. This cooked pasta resembles miniature derby hats and is Italian for "little ears."

8 ounces orecchiette or fusilli

One 15-ounce can chickpeas, drained

One 15-ounce can red kidney beans or black-eyed peas, drained

4 scallions, trimmed and chopped

2 large tomatoes, diced

1 cup frozen whole kernel corn, thawed

3 or 4 cloves garlic, minced

3 tablespoons olive oil or canola oil

3 tablespoons balsamic vinegar

¼ cup chopped fresh parsley

2 teaspoons dried oregano

½ teaspoon freshly ground black pepper

½ teaspoon salt

In a large saucepan, bring 3 quarts of water to a boil over medium-high heat. Place the pasta in the boiling water, stir, and return to a boil. Cook until al dente, 8 to 10 minutes, stirring occasionally. Drain in a colander and cool under cold running water.

Meanwhile, combine the remaining ingredients in a large mixing bowl and mix well. Fold in the cooked pasta. Refrigerate the salad for 15 minutes before serving. (The salad may be made up to one day in advance.)

When ready, serve the salad over a bed of leaf lettuce if desired.

Makes 6 servings

Per Serving:
360 Calories; 13g Protein; 9g Fat; 60g Carbohydrates; 0 Cholesterol; 503mg Sodium; 9g Fiber.

Pasta Vegetable Cobb Salad

Use freshly cooked or leftover pasta to make this in a hurry. This colorful salad may be prepared up to eight hours before serving. Drizzle with dressing and toss just before serving.

4 ounces (about 1½ cups) wheat-free corn or tri-colored corn pasta
8 ounces assorted torn salad greens (6 cups packed)
8 ounces (½ can) kidney beans or red beans, rinsed and drained
1 large tomato, seeded and diced
¾ cup frozen whole kernel corn, thawed
½ cup julienned or diced, drained, canned or bottled beets
½ cup diced red onion
½ cup (2 ounces) crumbled Gorgonzola cheese (optional)
½ cup fat-free or reduced-fat Italian salad dressing
Freshly ground black pepper

Cook the pasta according to the package directions. Drain; rinse with cold water, and drain again.

Meanwhile, arrange the greens on a large serving platter or in a large, shallow bowl. Arrange the beans, tomato, corn, beets, red onion, and cheese (if desired) in rows over the greens.

Arrange the pasta down center of greens. Drizzle with the dressing; toss just before serving. Garnish with pepper.

Makes 6 servings

Per Serving:
216 Calories; 6g Protein; 1g Fat; 47g Carbohydrates; 0 Cholesterol; 338mg Sodium; 9g Fiber.

Curried Vegetable Pasta Salad

*Many supermarket salad bars sell a mixture of diced colored bell peppers,
which helps to get this recipe on the table in thirty minutes.*

**8 ounces medium-sized
conchiglie or penne**
⅓ cup low-fat mayonnaise
¼ cup prepared mango chutney
1 teaspoon curry powder
¼ teaspoon salt, or to taste
⅛ teaspoon cayenne pepper
**1½ cups diced, mixed bell
peppers**
¾ cup frozen peas, thawed
**½ cup thinly sliced scallions or
chopped chives**
Spinach leaves (optional)
¼ cup chopped cilantro
**¼ cup sliced almonds, toasted
(optional; see Helpful Hint,
page 71)**

In a large saucepan, bring 3 quarts
of water to a boil over medium-
high heat. Place the pasta in the
boiling water, stir, and return
to a boil. Cook until al dente, 8 to
10 minutes, stirring occasionally.

While the pasta cooks, in a
large bowl, combine the mayonnaise, chutney, curry, salt, and
cayenne; mix well. Add the bell
peppers, peas, and scallions or
chives; toss to combine.

Drain the pasta in a colander,
rinse with cold water, and drain
again. Add the pasta to the bowl
with the bell pepper mixture and
toss well.

Serve the salad on a bed of
spinach leaves, if desired. Sprinkle
with cilantro, and, if desired,
almonds.

Makes 4 servings

Helpful Hint

*If the salad is refrigerated, the
dressing may thicken. Before
serving, thin with a tablespoon or
so of milk.*

Per Serving:
294 Calories; 6g Protein; 8g Fat;
50g Carbohydrates; 0 Cholesterol;
307mg Sodium; 5g Fiber.

Japanese-Style Udon Noodles

Udon noodles are flat Japanese noodles made from wheat or corn and are available dried and fresh in Asian groceries and in the Asian food section of most supermarkets.

8 ounces udon noodles
2 tablespoons tamari or
   soy sauce
2 tablespoons mirin
   (see Helpful Hint)
2 teaspoons dark or "toasted"
   sesame oil
½ cup diagonally sliced
   scallions

Cook the noodles according to package directions.

Meanwhile, in a large bowl, combine the tamari or soy sauce, mirin, and sesame oil. Drain the noodles, and transfer to the bowl with the tamari mixture. Add the scallions and toss well. Serve immediately.

Makes 4 servings

Helpful Hint

Mirin is Japanese rice wine, available in supermarkets, natural food stores, and Asian groceries.

Per Serving:
243 Calories; 9g Protein; 3g Fat;
45g Carbohydrates; 0 Cholesterol;
1,036mg Sodium; 2g Fiber.

Lemon-Thyme Summer Pasta Salad

8 ounces whole wheat or regular ziti, gemelli, or elbow macaroni

3 cups (about ¾ pound) 1-inch pieces fresh green beans

3 tablespoons garlic-infused olive oil, or 3 tablespoons extra virgin olive oil plus 1 teaspoon minced garlic

3 tablespoons fresh lemon juice

2 tablespoons fresh thyme leaves or 2 teaspoons dried

½ teaspoon salt, or to taste

½ teaspoon freshly ground black pepper

Fresh watercress or radicchio leaves (optional)

In a large saucepan, bring 3 quarts of water to a boil over medium-high heat. Place the pasta in the boiling water, stir, and return to a boil. Cook until al dente, 8 to 10 minutes, stirring occasionally, adding the green beans during last 5 to 6 minutes of cooking.

Meanwhile, in a large bowl, combine the oil, lemon juice, thyme, salt, and pepper. Drain the pasta and green beans in a colander, and add them to the bowl with the dressing; toss well.

Serve immediately over watercress or radicchio if desired, or cover and chill.

Makes 6 servings

Per Serving:
216 Calories; 7g Protein; 7g Fat; 34g Carbohydrates; 0 Cholesterol; 207mg Sodium; 2g Fiber.

Sesame Soba Noodles with Broccoli Rabe

*The slightly bitter flavor of broccoli rabe, also called rapini, is comple-
mented by the sweet wine in this easy side dish, which also is delicious
when served at room temperature.*

8 ounces soba or udon noodles

**1 bunch (about 1¼ pounds)
broccoli rabe, cut into
½-inch pieces, or 4 cups
broccoli florets**

**3 tablespoons tamari or soy
sauce**

**1 tablespoon dark or "toasted"
sesame oil**

**1 tablespoon mirin (Japanese
rice wine)**

**½ teaspoon hot chili oil
(optional)**

**2 teaspoons toasted sesame
seeds (see Helpful Hint,
page 71)**

In a large saucepan, bring 3 quarts
of water to a boil over medium-
high heat. Place the noodles in the
boiling water, stir, and return to a
boil. Cook until al dente, about
6 minutes, stirring occasionally,
adding broccoli rabe during last
3 minutes of cooking time.

Meanwhile, combine tamari or
soy sauce, sesame oil, mirin, and
chili oil (if desired) in a large
bowl.

Drain the noodles and broccoli
rabe in a colander, reserving 2
tablespoons of the pasta cooking
water. Add the noodles, broccoli
rabe, and reserved water to the
tamari mixture, and toss well.
Sprinkle with sesame seeds, and
serve hot or at room temperature.

Makes 6 servings

Per Serving:
199 Calories; 7g Protein; 4g Fat;
35g Carbohydrates; 0 Cholesterol;
384mg Sodium; 5g Fiber.

Cucumber Bow Tie Salad

**4 ounces bow tie pasta
(farfalle)**
2 tablespoons rice vinegar
**1½ tablespoons peanut or
vegetable oil**
1 teaspoon sugar
1 teaspoon hot chili oil
¼ teaspoon salt, or to taste
**1 small cucumber, scored,
thinly sliced (about 2 cups)**
½ cup chopped red bell pepper
**⅓ cup very thinly sliced red or
other sweet onion**

In a large saucepan, bring 3 quarts of water to a boil over medium-high heat. Place the pasta in the boiling water, stir, and return to a boil. Cook until al dente, 8 to 10 minutes, stirring occasionally.

Meanwhile, in a medium bowl, combine the vinegar, oil, sugar, chili oil, and salt; mix well. Add the cucumber, bell pepper, and onion, and toss to coat.

Drain the pasta in a colander, and rinse it with cold water to stop the cooking. Drain again, add to the cucumber mixture, and toss well. Serve immediately or cover and chill.

Makes 6 servings

Per Serving:
206 Calories; 6g Protein; 5g Fat;
35g Carbohydrates; 0 Cholesterol;
100mg Sodium; 3g Fiber.

Roasted Bell Pepper and Basil Salad

This salad is a huge hit during the summertime,
when bell peppers and basil are fresh and abundant.

**4 ounces regular fusilli or
tricolored fusilli**
1 red bell pepper
1 yellow bell pepper
**2 tablespoons extra-virgin
olive oil**
1 tablespoon balsamic vinegar
1 large clove garlic, minced
¼ teaspoon salt, or to taste
**¼ teaspoon freshly ground
black pepper**
**⅓ cup julienned, fresh basil
leaves**
**Crumbled goat cheese
(optional)**

In a large saucepan, bring 3 quarts of water to a boil over medium-high heat. Place the pasta in the boiling water, stir, and return to a boil. Cook until al dente, 8 to 10 minutes, stirring occasionally.

Meanwhile, preheat the broiler. Quarter the bell peppers lengthwise, discarding the stems and seeds. Place pepper quarters on a foil-lined baking sheet. Broil 3 to 4 inches from the heat source until the peppers are evenly charred, 10 to 12 minutes. Remove the peppers from the broiler, wrap them in the foil from the pan, and let them stand 5 minutes. (Alternatively, use 2 cups bottled, roasted red and yellow bell peppers: Rinse, drain, and slice the bottled peppers, and add ¼ teaspoon sugar to the dressing.)

Meanwhile, in a medium bowl, combine the oil, vinegar, garlic, salt, and pepper; mix well. Unwrap the peppers; pour any pepper juices from the foil into the dressing.

Peel off and discard the charred pepper skins, and slice the peppers crosswise into ¼-inch strips. Add the pepper strips to the dressing.

Drain the pasta in a colander; rinse the pasta with cold water to stop cooking and drain again. Add the pasta to the pepper mixture. Add the basil, and toss well. Serve immediately or cover and chill. Sprinkle with goat cheese just before serving, if desired.

Makes 4 servings

Per Serving:
256 Calories; 6g Protein; 8g Fat;
41g Carbohydrates; 0 Cholesterol;
154mg Sodium; 3g Fiber.

Picnic Pasta Salad

*As its name says, this is a perfect salad for a picnic—
it's easy to make and travels well.*

7 ounces (2 cups dry) ditalini, conchigliette piccole, or elbow macaroni
⅓ cup low-fat or reduced-fat mayonnaise
1½ tablespoons Dijon or "country Dijon" mustard
1 teaspoon bottled horseradish
1 cup red and yellow cherry tomatoes (halved if large), or yellow pear tomatoes
½ cup sliced scallions
2 hard-cooked eggs, chopped (optional)
Red leaf lettuce leaves (optional)

In a large saucepan, bring 3 quarts of water to a boil over medium-high heat. Place the pasta in the boiling water, stir, and return to a boil. Cook until al dente, 8 to 10 minutes, stirring occasionally.

Meanwhile, in a large bowl, combine the mayonnaise, mustard, and horseradish; mix well.

Drain the pasta in a colander. Rinse it with cold water to stop the cooking and drain again. Add the pasta to the mayonnaise mixture, and toss to coat. Add the tomatoes, scallions, and eggs if desired; toss well. Serve immediately on leaves of lettuce if desired, or cover and chill until serving time.

Makes 6 servings

Per Serving:
186 Calories; 5g Protein; 5g Fat; 29g Carbohydrates; 1mg Cholesterol; 124mg Sodium; 1g Fiber.

Tubetti Hawaiian Salad

Tubetti are tiny, tubelike pasta shapes.
Substitute baby penne pasta if necessary.

6 ounces tubetti or baby penne
1 ripe papaya or 2 ripe mangoes
2 tablespoons vegetable oil
2 tablespoons unsweetened
    pineapple juice
2 tablespoons fresh lime juice
2 teaspoons bottled, minced,
    red jalapeño peppers or 1
    jalapeño or serrano pepper,
    seeded and minced
¼ teaspoon salt, or to taste
½ cup chopped red bell pepper
½ cup chopped cilantro

In a large saucepan, bring 3 quarts of water to a boil over medium-high heat. Place the pasta in the boiling water, stir, and return to a boil. Cook until al dente, 8 to 10 minutes, stirring occasionally.

Meanwhile, peel, seed, and cut the papaya or mangoes into ¹/₂-inch pieces; set aside.

In a large bowl, combine the oil, pineapple juice, lime juice, jalapeños, and salt; mix well.

Drain the pasta in a colander; rinse with cold water to stop the cooking. Add the pasta to the bowl with the dressing and toss well. Add the papaya or mangoes, bell pepper, and cilantro; toss again. Serve immediately at room temperature.

Makes 4 servings

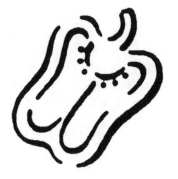

Per Serving:
247 Calories; 6g Protein; 8g Fat;
40g Carbohydrates; 0 Cholesterol;
171mg Sodium; 4g Fiber.

Ditalini Succotash

Here is an Italian-inspired variation of this traditional native American dish. The short, tubular shape of ditalini pasta blends well with lima beans and corn.

One 10-ounce package frozen lima beans (about 2 cups)
½ cup ditalini
2 teaspoons canola oil
1 small onion, finely chopped
1 red or green bell pepper, seeded and diced
2 cloves garlic, minced
1½ cups corn kernels, fresh or frozen
One 14-ounce can stewed tomatoes
1 teaspoon dried oregano
½ teaspoon ground black pepper
½ teaspoon salt

In a large saucepan, bring 3 quarts of water to a boil over medium-high heat. Place the lima beans in the boiling water, stir, and return to a rapid boil. Stir in the ditalini, and cook over medium-high heat until al dente, 8 to 10 minutes, stirring occasionally. Drain the beans and pasta in a colander.

Meanwhile, in a medium saucepan, heat the oil over medium-high heat. Add the onion, bell pepper, and garlic and cook, stirring, for 5 to 6 minutes. Add all of the remaining ingredients, and cook for 7 to 10 minutes over medium heat, stirring occasionally.

Stir the cooked lima beans and ditalini into the corn-and-tomato mixture and cook for 5 minutes more over medium heat, stirring occasionally. Serve the succotash as a hearty side dish.

Makes 6 servings

Per Serving:
183 Calories; 7g Protein; 2g Fat; 35g Carbohydrates; 0 Cholesterol; 486mg Sodium; 3g Fiber.

Rice Noodle Salad with Peanut Dressing

*In Asian cuisine, rice noodles and peanut dressings go hand-in-hand.
The noodles are flexible enough to hold the peanut butter–based dressing,
but still delicate enough to melt in your mouth.*

**8 to 10 ounces rice vermicelli or
    rice sticks**
¼ cup chunky peanut butter
¼ cup low-sodium soy sauce
**2 tablespoons mirin (Japanese
    rice wine)**
2 tablespoons water
**2 teaspoons minced fresh
    gingerroot**
4 ounces extra-firm tofu, diced
**4 whole scallions, trimmed and
    chopped**
**½ cup diced roasted red bell
    peppers**
**2 tablespoons chopped fresh
    cilantro or Thai basil
    (optional)**

In a large saucepan, bring 3 quarts of water to a boil. Place the noodles in boiling water and cook until al dente, stirring occasionally, 4 to 5 minutes. Drain in a colander and cool under cold running water.

Meanwhile, place the peanut butter, soy sauce, mirin, water, and ginger in a blender or a food processor fitted with a steel blade and process until smooth, about 5 seconds. Transfer the dressing to a medium mixing bowl. Add the cooked noodles and remaining ingredients and toss together thoroughly. Serve immediately or refrigerate for later.

Makes 4 servings

Per Serving:
347 Calories; 14g Protein; 8g Fat;
50g Carbohydrates; 0 Cholesterol;
612mg Sodium; 4g Fiber.

Fragrant Thai Cellophane Noodle Salad

*The aromatic flavors of Thai cooking—lime, ginger, and cilantro—
infuse the mildly flavored cellophane noodles with a fragrant
personality. Soy sauce makes an adequate substitute for the traditional
(but odoriferous) Thai fish sauce.*

**4 ounces cellophane noodles
(Chinese vermicelli)**
**¼ pound extra-firm tofu,
cut into ¼-inch-wide
matchsticks**
**4 whole scallions, trimmed and
chopped**
4 radishes, thinly sliced
**1 medium cucumber, peeled
and diced**
2 ounces mung bean sprouts
**2 teaspoons minced fresh
gingerroot**
¼ cup low-sodium soy sauce
1 tablespoon peanut oil
2 teaspoons dark brown sugar
**1 teaspoon dark or "toasted"
sesame oil**
Juice of 1 lime
**2 or 3 tablespoons chopped
cilantro**

In a large saucepan, bring 3 quarts
of water to a boil. Place the
noodles in boiling water and turn
off the heat. Let the noodles soak
until al dente, stirring occasionally, 4 to 5 minutes. Drain in a
colander and cool under cold
running water.

Meanwhile, in a large mixing
bowl, combine all of the remaining ingredients and blend together thoroughly. Add the
noodles and toss well. Serve as a
salad or side dish.

Makes 4 servings

Helpful Hint

*For more spice, add 2 or 3 table-
spoons chopped Thai basil leaves
and 1 hot pepper, seeded and
minced.*

Per Serving:
218 Calories; 10g Protein; 7g Fat;
30g Carbohydrates; 0 Cholesterol;
1,233mg Sodium; 2g Fiber.

Garden Bow Tie Pasta with Basil-Balsamic Vinaigrette

Bow tie pasta (also called farfalle) adds a playful touch to the pasta salad genre. The herbal dressing for the salad is enhanced with balsamic vinegar, a well-aged grape vinegar with a smooth, mildly tart flavor.

8 ounces bow tie pasta (farfalle)
3 tablespoons canola oil
3 tablespoons balsamic vinegar
2 teaspoons Dijon mustard
2 cloves garlic, minced
½ cup mixed fresh herbs, chopped (such as parsley, basil, and oregano)
2 teaspoons dried oregano
½ teaspoon freshly ground black pepper
½ teaspoon salt
12 to 14 cherry tomatoes, halved
4 whole scallions, trimmed chopped
1 yellow or red bell pepper (preferably roasted), diced
2 cups coarsely chopped spinach
One 15-ounce can chickpeas, drained
⅓ to ½ cup freshly grated Parmesan cheese

In a large saucepan, bring 2½ quarts of water to a boil over medium-high heat. Place the bow ties in the boiling water, stir, and return to a boil. Cook, stirring occasionally, until al dente, 10 to 12 minutes. Drain in a colander and cool under cold running water.

Meanwhile, in a large mixing bowl, whisk together the oil, vinegar, mustard, garlic, herbs, oregano, pepper, and salt. Add the cooked pasta, tomatoes, scallions, bell pepper, spinach, and chickpeas and blend well. Fold in the Parmesan cheese.

Serve immediately or refrigerate for later.

Makes 6 servings

Per Serving:
303 Calories; 10g Protein; 10g Fat; 45g Carbohydrates; 3mg Cholesterol; 321mg Sodium; 6g Fiber.

Yellow Orzo Pilaf

Orzo's elliptical shape makes it a natural companion to rice in salads, pilafs, and one-pot dishes.

1 tablespoon olive oil
1 medium yellow onion, chopped
2 cloves garlic, minced
1 cup long grain white rice or parboiled rice
½ cup orzo
½ teaspoon salt
½ teaspoon freshly ground black pepper
¼ teaspoon curry powder
2¾ cups water
1 cup cooked (or canned) and drained chickpeas
2 tablespoons chopped fresh parsley

In a medium saucepan, heat the oil over medium heat. Add the onion and garlic and cook, stirring, for 4 minutes. Stir in the rice, orzo, salt, pepper, and curry, reduce the heat to low and cook for 1 minute, stirring frequently. Add the water and chickpeas and bring to a simmer over high heat. Reduce the heat to low, cover, and cook until all of the liquid is absorbed, 15 to 20 minutes.

Remove from the heat, fluff the grains with a fork, and blend in the parsley. Let stand, covered, for 5 to 10 minutes before serving.

Makes 4 servings

Per Serving:
327 Calories; 9g Protein; 5g Fat; 51g Carbohydrates; 0 Cholesterol; 298mg Sodium; 2g Fiber.

Tricolored Pasta Salad
with Artichokes and Goat Cheese

Artichokes and goat cheese imbue this salad with mellifluous flavors and smooth textures. When in season, edible flowers (such as nasturtiums or pansies) contribute to the sophisticated nature of this dish.

8 ounces tricolored rotini
2 tablespoons canola oil
¼ cup red wine vinegar
2 teaspoons Dijon mustard
¼ cup chopped fresh parsley
2 cloves garlic, minced
½ teaspoon freshly ground
  black pepper
½ teaspoon salt
12 yellow or red cherry toma-
  toes, halved
4 whole scallions, trimmed and
  chopped
One 14-ounce can artichoke
  hearts, drained and
  coarsely chopped
½ cup diced roasted sweet red
  peppers
1 dozen nasturtium flowers,
  rinsed (optional)
2 ounces goat cheese (chèvre)

In a large saucepan, bring 2½ quarts of water to a boil over medium-high heat. Place the rotini in the boiling water, stir, and return to a boil. Cook until al dente, 9 to 11 minutes. Drain in a colander; cool quickly under cold running water.

Meanwhile, in a large mixing bowl, whisk together the oil, vinegar, mustard, parsley, garlic, pepper, and salt. Add the rotini, tomatoes, scallions, artichokes, roasted peppers, and nasturtiums (if desired) and stir together. Gently fold in the goat cheese. If possible, chill for about 1 hour before serving.

Makes 6 servings

Per Serving:
243 Calories; 8g Protein; 7g Fat; 36g Carbohydrates; 8mg Cholesterol; 374mg Sodium; 6g Fiber.

Southwestern Tortellini Salad with Black Beans and Corn

This colorful, offbeat pasta salad is heightened with the signature flavors of Southwestern cuisine—cilantro, cumin, lime, and chilies. It makes a satisfying picnic or lunch entrée.

8 ounces cheese tortellini (dried, not frozen)
2 tablespoons canola oil
Juice of 2 limes
¼ cup chopped cilantro
3 to 4 cloves garlic, minced
1 to 2 jalapeño peppers, seeded and minced
1½ teaspoons ground cumin
½ teaspoon freshly ground black pepper
½ teaspoon salt
2 tomatoes, diced
One 15-ounce can black beans, drained
1½ cups cooked corn kernels, fresh, canned, or frozen
4 whole scallions, trimmed and chopped
1 green bell pepper, seeded and diced

In a large saucepan, bring 2½ quarts of water to a boil over medium-high heat. Place the tortellini in the boiling water, stir, and return to a boil. Cook, stirring occasionally, until al dente, 12 to 15 minutes. Drain the pasta in a colander and cool under cold running water.

Meanwhile, in a large mixing bowl, whisk together the oil, lime juice, cilantro, garlic, jalapeños, cumin, pepper, and salt. Stir in the cooked tortellini and the remaining ingredients. Refrigerate for 1 hour before serving (allowing the flavors to mingle). Fluff the salad with a fork before serving.

Makes 6 servings

Per Serving:
259 Calories; 11g Protein; 8g Fat; 42g Carbohydrates; 20mg Cholesterol; 674mg Sodium; 7g Fiber.

Caesar-Style Pasta Salad

Cooking the garlic cloves in the pasta water gives the garlic a sweet, nutty flavor.

8 ounces cavatappi or cavatelli
4 cloves garlic, peeled
2 tablespoons low-fat mayonnaise
2 tablespoons olive oil
1 tablespoon fresh lemon juice
2 teaspoons Dijon or hot Dijon mustard
¼ teaspoon salt
¼ teaspoon freshly ground black pepper
8 cups packed, sliced (½ inch thick) romaine lettuce leaves
¼ cup freshly grated Parmesan cheese
1½ cups prepared garlic croutons (optional)

In a large saucepan, bring 3 quarts of water to a boil over medium-high heat. Place the pasta and garlic cloves in the boiling water, stir, and return to a boil. Cook until al dente, 8 to 10 minutes, stirring occasionally.

Meanwhile, in a small bowl, whisk together the mayonnaise, oil, lemon juice, mustard, salt, and pepper.

Drain the pasta and garlic; rinse with cold water to stop the cooking. Mince or mash the cooked garlic cloves with a fork, and whisk into the mayonnaise mixture.

In a large bowl, combine the lettuce, pasta, and mayonnaise mixture. Toss well to coat; transfer to 8 chilled salad plates. Sprinkle with cheese and, if desired, croutons. Serve with additional freshly ground black pepper, if desired.

Makes 8 servings

Per Serving:
183 Calories; 6g Protein; 6g Fat; 26g Carbohydrates; 3mg Cholesterol; 161mg Sodium; 3g Fiber.

Greek Orzo Salad

1½ cups (10 ounces) orzo
¼ cup olive oil
3 tablespoons fresh lemon juice
3 tablespoons chopped mint leaves or 1 tablespoon dried mint
2 tablespoons chopped basil leaves or 2 teaspoons dried basil
1 tablespoon white balsamic or white wine vinegar
2 cloves garlic, minced
¾ teaspoon salt
½ teaspoon freshly ground black pepper
2 large tomatoes, seeded and diced, or 16 cherry tomatoes, halved
1 small cucumber, scored, sliced, slices halved (1½ cups)
½ cup bottled, drained, roasted red bell pepper strips
4 ounces feta or goat cheese, crumbled (optional)
½ cup pitted, halved kalamata olives (optional)
Romaine lettuce leaves
Mint sprigs (optional)

In a large saucepan, bring 3 quarts of water to a boil over medium-high heat. Place the orzo in the boiling water, stir, and return to a boil. Cook until al dente, 7 to 8 minutes, stirring occasionally.

Meanwhile, combine the oil, lemon juice, mint, basil, vinegar, garlic, salt, and pepper in a large bowl; mix well.

Drain the orzo; rinse with cold water and drain again. Add to the bowl with mint mixture; toss well.

Add the tomatoes, cucumber, and bell peppers; toss again. Add the cheese and olives, if desired; toss again. Serve on lettuce leaves, garnished with mint sprigs, if desired.

Makes 8 servings

Per Serving:
163 Calories; 3g Protein; 7g Fat; 22g Carbohydrates; 0 Cholesterol; 224mg Sodium; 2g Fiber.

Sesame Noodle Pancake

*Use this tasty noodle pancake in place of rice as a base
for stir-fries or ragouts.*

**One 5-ounce package chuka
soba (Chinese or Japanese
curly noodles)**
**1½ tablespoons tamari or
regular soy sauce**
**3 teaspoons dark or "toasted"
sesame oil**

In a large saucepan, bring 3 quarts of water to a boil over medium-high heat. Place the noodles in the boiling water, stir, and return to a boil. Cook until al dente, 8 to 10 minutes, stirring occasionally. Drain well; return to pot. Add the tamari or soy sauce and toss well.

Heat 1½ teaspoons of the oil in a 12-inch nonstick skillet over medium heat until hot. Add the noodles; pat into an even layer with a spatula. Cook until the bottom of the noodles is lightly browned, 6 to 7 minutes. Invert onto a plate.

Add the remaining 1½ teaspoons of the oil to the skillet; slide pancake back into skillet, browned side up. Continue cooking 6 to 7 minutes or until bottom is well browned. Cut into quarters.

Makes 4 servings

Per Serving:
159 Calories; 6g Protein; 4g Fat;
26g Carbohydrates; 33mg Cholesterol; 384mg Sodium; 1g Fiber.

Moroccan Rotini

8 ounces whole wheat or
    regular rotini
1 tablespoon olive oil
1 large onion, chopped
4 cloves garlic, minced
1 cup vegetable broth
½ teaspoon crushed saffron
    threads (see Helpful Hint,
    page 58) or ground
    turmeric
½ teaspoon paprika (preferably
    sweet Hungarian)
¼ teaspoon salt, or to taste
¼ teaspoon ground cumin
¼ teaspoon ground gingerroot
¼ teaspoon hot paprika or
    cayenne pepper
⅓ cup golden or dark raisins
1 tablespoon water
1 teaspoon cornstarch
⅓ cup coarsely chopped
    cilantro
¼ cup sliced almonds, toasted
    (optional; see Helpful Hint,
    page 71)

In a large saucepan, bring 3 quarts of water to a boil over medium-high heat. Place the pasta in the boiling water, stir, and return to a boil. Cook until al dente, 9 to 11 minutes, stirring occasionally.

Meanwhile, heat the oil in a large skillet over medium heat. Add the onion and garlic and cook, stirring, for 5 minutes.

Add the broth, saffron or turmeric, paprika, salt, cumin, ginger, and hot paprika or cayenne; bring to a boil, stirring frequently. Add the raisins, reduce the heat to low, and simmer, uncovered, 5 minutes.

Combine the water and cornstarch in a cup, mixing until smooth. Stir into the broth mixture, and simmer until the sauce thickens, about 1 minute, stirring occasionally.

Drain the pasta, and add it to the skillet, tossing until the pasta is lightly coated with sauce. Stir in the cilantro; sprinkle with almonds, if desired.

Makes 4 servings

Per Serving:
288 Calories; 10g Protein; 6g Fat; 57g Carbohydrates; 0 Cholesterol; 405mg Sodium; 1g Fiber.

Confetti Ditalini Salad

Ditalini makes a delicious couscous-like salad. Colorful carrots, radishes, scallions, corn, and a squeeze of tangy citrus fruit complete the picture. Unlike the tiny couscous grains, you can actually bite into ditalini.

2 cups ditalini
4 whole scallions, trimmed
    and chopped
4 radishes, chopped
1 large carrot, shredded
1 cup cooked corn kernels
    (about one 11-ounce can)
2 tablespoons olive oil or
    canola oil
Juice of 2 limes or lemons
2 tablespoons chopped fresh
    parsley
½ teaspoon freshly ground
    black pepper
½ teaspoon salt

In a large saucepan, bring 4 quarts of water to a boil over medium-high heat. Place the pasta in the boiling water, stir, and return to a boil. Cook until al dente, 5 to 7 minutes, stirring occasionally. Drain the pasta in a colander and cool under cold running water.

Meanwhile, combine the remaining ingredients in a large mixing bowl and blend well. Fold in the cooked pasta. Refrigerate the salad for 10 to 15 minutes before serving. (The salad may be made up to one day ahead of time.)

Serve the salad over a bed of leaf lettuce.

Makes 4 servings

Per Serving:
325 Calories; 9g Protein; 8g Fat; 55g Carbohydrates; 0 Cholesterol; 436mg Sodium; 3g Fiber.

CHAPTER 3

Sauces

Tomato-Vodka Sauce

A classic sauce.

1½ tablespoons olive oil
½ cup chopped shallots or
    sweet onion
⅓ cup vodka
1 cup canned evaporated
    skim milk
One 15-ounce can tomato sauce
⅛ teaspoon cayenne pepper
    (optional)

Heat the oil in a heavy, large skillet over medium heat. Add the shallots or onion, and cook, stirring, for 4 minutes.

Add the vodka; carefully ignite the sauce with a long match (the flame will extinguish in about 1 minute). Reduce the heat to low and simmer 2 minutes, shaking pan occasionally.

Add the milk, and simmer, stirring frequently, until the sauce is reduced and has thickened, about 10 minutes. Add the tomato sauce and cayenne, if desired, and simmer until thickened again, about 5 minutes more.

Serve immediately over hot pasta, or store, covered, in refrigerator, for up to 3 days.

Makes about 2 cups,
or four ½-cup servings

Per Serving:
173 Calories; 6g Protein; 5g Fat;
16g Carbohydrates; 2mg Cholesterol;
769mg Sodium; 2g Fiber.

Fresh Tomato Marinara

This is a tomato lover's sauce. Juicy, ripe garden tomatoes, pungent garlic, and vibrant summer herbs conspire to form a delectable and versatile creation.

8 large ripe tomatoes, coarsely chopped
2 tablespoons olive oil
1 medium red onion, chopped
4 cloves garlic, minced
1 teaspoon salt
½ teaspoon freshly ground black pepper
¼ cup chopped fresh basil
¼ cup chopped fresh parsley
2 teaspoons honey
Freshly grated Parmesan cheese to taste (optional)

Place the tomatoes in a colander and let drain for about 1 minute. Stir the tomatoes around once or twice with a large spoon.

In a large saucepan, heat the oil over medium-high heat. Add the onion and garlic and cook, stirring, for 3 minutes. Add the tomatoes, salt, and pepper, and cook over medium heat, stirring occasionally, until the tomatoes become thick and saucelike, 15 to 20 minutes. Remove from the heat and let cool slightly.

Transfer the tomatoes to a blender or a food processor, and process until smooth, 10 seconds. Return the sauce to the pan and blend in the basil, parsley, and honey.

Ladle the sauce over cooked pasta; if desired, offer grated Parmesan cheese as a garnish.

Makes 3½ cups, or seven ½-cup servings

Per Serving:
82 Calories; 2g Protein; 4g Fat; 11g Carbohydrates; 0 Cholesterol; 347mg Sodium; 2g Fiber.

Piquant Creole Red Sauce

Creole sauce is the "marinara" of Louisiana. It has a peppery personality and religiously includes bell pepper, onion, and celery—the holy trinity of Creole cooking. Serve the sauce with large noodles, such as rigatoni, fettuccine, or shells.

1 tablespoon canola oil
1 green bell pepper, seeded
    and diced
1 medium yellow onion, diced
1 stalk celery, diced
2 cloves garlic, minced
One 28-ounce can
    crushed tomatoes
½ cup water or vegetable broth
2 teaspoons dried oregano
1½ teaspoons dried thyme
½ teaspoon salt
½ teaspoon black pepper
¼ teaspoon cayenne pepper
1 to 2 teaspoons bottled
    hot pepper sauce
    (such as Tabasco)

In a large saucepan, heat the oil over medium heat. Add the bell pepper, onion, celery, and garlic, and cook, stirring, for 8 minutes. Add all of the remaining ingredients, and cook over medium-low heat for 15 to 20 minutes, stirring occasionally.

Remove from the heat and let stand for 5 to 10 minutes. Ladle the sauce over cooked pasta or refrigerate for later.

**Makes 5 cups,
or ten ½-cup servings**

Per Serving:
29 Calories; 1g Protein; 2g Fat;
4g Carbohydrates; 0 Cholesterol;
190mg Sodium; 1g Fiber.

Alfredo Sauce Redux

Alfredo sauce is an Italian cream sauce typically served with fettuccine. Unfortunately, traditional Alfredo is prepared with lots of butter, heavy cream, egg yolks, and cheese—and dripping with artery-clogging fat. This healthful improvisation captures the creamy mouth feel and flavor of Alfredo, but contains dramatically less calories and fat.

2 teaspoons olive oil or canola oil
1 small yellow onion, chopped
2 cloves garlic, minced
2 cups low-fat milk (1 percent or 2 percent)
¼ cup freshly chopped parsley
½ teaspoon white pepper
1 teaspoon salt (see Helpful Hint)
1 tablespoon cornstarch
1 tablespoon cold water
⅓ cup shredded low-fat cheese, such as mozzarella or Swiss

In a medium saucepan, heat the oil over medium heat. Add the onion and garlic and cook, stirring, for 2 to 3 minutes. Stir in the milk, parsley, white pepper, and salt, and bring to a gentle simmer over medium heat

Meanwhile, in a small mixing bowl, combine the cornstarch and water to form a paste. Stir the paste into the simmering white sauce and return to a gentle simmer. Cook for about 1 minute more over low heat, stirring frequently. Whisk in the cheese.

Immediately ladle the sauce over servings of cooked pasta.

Makes 2 cups, or four ½-cup servings

Helpful Hint

For a low-sodium version, add the juice of 1 lemon to the sauce a few minutes before serving and cut back on the salt.

Per Serving:
123 Calories; 8g Protein; 5g Fat; 12g Carbohydrates; 9mg Cholesterol; 665mg Sodium; 1g Fiber.

Versatile Vinaigrette for Pasta Salad

This smooth-and-tart vinaigrette breathes life into a bowl of cold noodles. Once the pasta and dressing are tossed together, a variety of accoutrements can be added (such as canned beans, artichokes, steamed broccoli, roasted peppers, grated cheese, minced garlic, scallions, and so forth). The dressing clings to the pasta without dominating matters.

¼ **cup canola oil**
2 tablespoons red wine vinegar
1 tablespoon balsamic vinegar
1½ teaspoons Dijon mustard
1 to 2 teaspoons honey
1 teaspoon dried oregano
½ **teaspoon each of dried basil**
    and thyme
½ **teaspoon freshly ground**
    black pepper
½ **teaspoon salt**
¼ **cup chopped fresh basil or**
    parsley (optional)

Combine all of the ingredients in a mixing bowl and whisk thoroughly. (Or combine in a jar with a tight-fitting lid and shake well.) Refrigerate for 15 to 30 minutes to allow the flavors to develop.

Makes ½ cup, enough for
4 servings of pasta

Per Serving:
131 Calories; 0.7g Protein; 13g Fat; 3g Carbohydrates; 0 Cholesterol; 303mg Sodium; 0g Fiber.

Sicilian Red Sauce

Made from concentrated tomato paste, this garlicky red sauce is a paragon of purity, simplicity, and unpretentiousness. Serve it with long strands of pasta, such as spaghetti, capellini, or linguini.

2 tablespoons olive oil
4 cloves garlic, minced
Two 6-ounce cans tomato paste
4 cups water
2 teaspoons dried parsley
1 teaspoon dried basil
1 teaspoon sugar
½ teaspoon freshly ground
    black pepper
½ teaspoon salt

In a large saucepan, heat the oil over medium heat. Add the garlic and cook, stirring, for 2 minutes (do not burn). Add all of the remaining ingredients, and stir together until completely blended, forming a sauce. Bring the sauce to a simmer over medium-high heat, stirring frequently.

Reduce the heat to low and cook, uncovered, for 15 to 20 minutes, stirring occasionally. Remove the sauce from the heat and ladle over cooked noodles. (Freshly grated Parmesan cheese is a traditional accompaniment.)

**Makes 4 cups,
or eight ½-cup servings**

Per Serving:
57 Calories; 3g Protein; 2g Fat;
8g Carbohydrates; 0 Cholesterol;
171mg Sodium; 1g Fiber.

Classic Red Sauce

Red sauce (called gravy by some) can be a vegetarian's best friend. It is one of the few meatless sauces served in an Italian restaurant, and at home it is easy and quick to prepare. This version is enhanced with a trio of traditional Italian herbs: parsley, oregano, and basil.

1 tablespoon olive oil
1 medium yellow onion, diced
2 cloves garlic, minced
One 28-ounce can plum
   tomatoes
¼ cup chopped fresh parsley
1 teaspoon sugar (optional)
1 teaspoon dried oregano
1 teaspoon dried basil
½ teaspoon freshly ground
   black pepper
½ teaspoon salt

In a large saucepan, heat the oil over medium heat. Add the onion and garlic and cook, stirring, for 4 minutes. Add all remaining ingredients and bring to a simmer. Cook for 20 minutes over low heat, stirring occasionally.

Transfer the sauce to a blender or food processor fitted with a steel blade and process until smooth, for about 5 seconds. Return the sauce to the pan and keep warm until the pasta is ready.

**Makes 2 cups,
or four ½-cup servings**

Per Serving:
76 Calories; 2g Protein; 3g Fat;
9g Carbohydrates; 0 Cholesterol;
514mg Sodium; 2g Fiber.

Mint Pesto

Prepared in the Sicilian tradition, this pesto is a fragrant paste of almonds or walnuts, tomatoes, basil, mint, and of course, olive oil and grated Parmesan. It blends well with hot or cold pasta and can also be used by the tablespoon as a condiment.

4 to 6 cloves garlic
⅓ cup almonds or walnuts
2 juicy plum tomatoes, diced
1 cup fresh basil leaves,
  coarsely chopped
1 cup fresh mint leaves
⅓ cup olive oil
½ teaspoon salt
½ teaspoon freshly ground
  black pepper
¼ cup freshly grated
  Parmesan cheese

Add the garlic and nuts to a blender or a food processor fitted with a steel blade. Process for 5 to 10 seconds, stopping once to scrape the sides. Add the tomatoes, basil, mint, oil, salt, and pepper, and process until smooth, 5 to 10 seconds more. Stop at least once to scrape the sides. Transfer to a mixing bowl and fold in the cheese. Toss immediately with cooked pasta or refrigerate until ready to use.

Makes about 1½ cups

Per tablespoon:
42 Calories; 0.8g Protein; 4g Fat; 1g Carbohydrates; 0.7mg Cholesterol; 61mg Sodium; 0.4g Fiber.

Green Ricotta Sauce

This versatile sauce combines the creaminess of ricotta cheese with nutrient-dense leafy greens and verdant herbs. Serve the sauce with any shape or flavor of pasta, hot or cold.

2 teaspoons canola oil
1 small yellow onion, diced
2 cloves garlic, minced
8 cups coarsely chopped leafy greens (spinach, kale, or chard; see Helpful Hint)
½ cup coarsely chopped fresh basil or arugula
1 cup part-skim ricotta cheese
1 teaspoon salt
½ teaspoon freshly ground black pepper

In a large saucepan or wok, heat the oil over medium heat. Add the onion and garlic and cook, stirring, for 3 to 4 minutes. Add the greens and basil or arugula, and cook, stirring, until the greens are wilted, about 4 minutes. Transfer the greens mixture to a blender or a food processor fitted with a steel blade. Add the ricotta cheese, salt, and pepper, and process until smooth, about 5 seconds.

Combine the ricotta sauce with cooked pasta and serve immediately.

Makes 3 cups, or six ½-cup servings

Helpful Hint

Although 8 cups of leafy greens sounds imposing, the greens wilt down considerably when cooked. One 10-ounce package of spinach equals about 8 cups.

Per Serving:
95 Calories; 7g Protein; 5g Fat; 7g Carbohydrates; 13mg Cholesterol; 498mg Sodium; 2g Fiber.

Puttanesca Sauce

*Olives and capers make this quick-cooking traditional
Italian sauce very flavorful.*

1 tablespoon olive oil
1 large onion, chopped
4 cloves garlic, minced
Two 14½-ounce cans diced
   tomatoes, undrained
2 tablespoons tomato paste
2 teaspoons dried basil
¼ teaspoon red pepper flakes
¼ cup chopped, pitted
   kalamata olives
¼ cup chopped flat-leaf parsley
1 tablespoon drained capers

Heat the oil in a large saucepan
over medium heat. Add the onion,
and cook, stirring, for 8 minutes.
Add the garlic, and cook, stirring,
1 minute more. Stir in the tomatoes, tomato paste, basil, and
pepper flakes, and bring to a
simmer over high heat. Reduce the
heat to low, and simmer, uncovered, 10 minutes, stirring
occasionally.

Stir in olives, parsley, and
capers; continue to simmer 2 more
minutes. Serve over hot pasta.

**Makes about 4 cups,
or eight ½-cup servings**

Per Serving:
43 Calories; 1g Protein; 3g Fat;
5g Carbohydrates; 0 Cholesterol;
114mg Sodium; 1g Fiber.

Roasted Red Pepper Sauce

Bottled, roasted red peppers make this delicious sauce very quick to prepare. If you prefer a less tangy sauce and have the time to roast your own peppers, you may substitute 2½ cups roasted and peeled fresh red bell peppers for the bottled peppers and omit the sugar.

Two 12-ounce jars roasted red bell peppers, drained and rinsed

2 tablespoons olive oil (preferably extra-virgin)

3 cloves garlic, minced

⅓ cup prepared salsa or picante sauce

⅔ cup reduced-fat or regular sour cream

1 tablespoon all-purpose flour

¾ teaspoon sugar

¼ teaspoon salt

Pat rinsed peppers between paper towels; transfer to food processor. Process until peppers are finely chopped; set aside.

Heat oil in a medium saucepan over medium heat. Add garlic and cook, stirring, until the garlic is softened, but not brown, about 2 minutes. Add the chopped peppers and salsa, reduce the heat to medium-low, and simmer, uncovered, 5 minutes.

In a small bowl, combine sour cream and flour and mix well. Add to sauce with sugar and salt; reduce heat to low and cook 8 minutes, stirring frequently. The sauce may be served immediately, covered and refrigerated up to 3 days, or frozen up to 3 months.

Makes about 3 cups, or six ½-cup servings

Per Serving:
92 Calories; 2g Protein; 5g Fat; 10g Carbohydrates; 0 Cholesterol; 240mg Sodium; 1g Fiber.

Balsamic Marinara Sauce

*Balsamic vinegar gives this quick-cooking
marinara sauce a long-cooked flavor.*

2 tablespoons olive oil
1 large onion, finely chopped
4 cloves garlic, minced
One 28-ounce can pureed
**   tomatoes**
2 tablespoons balsamic vinegar
¼ teaspoon sugar, or to taste
½ teaspoon salt, or to taste

Heat oil in a large saucepan over medium-high heat. Add the onion, and cook, stirring, for 8 minutes. Add the garlic, and cook, stirring, 1 minute. Add all of the remaining ingredients, and bring to a simmer.

Reduce the heat to low and simmer, uncovered and stirring frequently, for 15 minutes. Serve over hot pasta. The sauce may be refrigerated up to 3 days or frozen up to 3 months.

**Makes about 4 cups,
or eight ½-cup servings**

Per Serving:
104 Calories; 2g Protein; 4g Fat;
18g Carbohydrates; 0 Cholesterol;
585mg Sodium; 3g Fiber.

Herbed Artichoke-Tomato Sauce

*Toss this quick and easy sauce with your favorite pasta
or use in Bistro Penne Rigate (page 42).*

1 tablespoon olive oil
3 cloves garlic, minced
Two 14½-ounce cans Italian-
    style diced tomatoes,
    undrained
One 6- to 8-ounce jar marinated
    artichoke hearts, drained,
    and coarsely chopped
¼ cup tomato paste
1 teaspoon dried basil leaves
1 teaspoon dried thyme leaves
½ teaspoon dried oregano
    leaves

Heat oil in a large saucepan over
medium heat. Add the garlic, and
cook, stirring, for 2 minutes. Add
the remaining ingredients and
bring to a simmer. Reduce the
heat to low and simmer, uncovered and stirring frequently, for
15 minutes. Serve over hot pasta.

**Makes about 3½ cups,
or seven ½-cup servings**

Per Serving:
49 Calories; 1g Protein; 4g Fat;
5g Carbohydrates; 0 Cholesterol;
103mg Sodium; 1g Fiber.

Roasted Garlic and Tomato Sauce

This quick broiler method of roasting garlic saves time
but doesn't skimp on flavor.

8 cloves garlic
4 ripe firm large tomatoes
(about 2¼ pounds)
2 tablespoons extra-virgin
olive oil
½ teaspoon salt
½ teaspoon freshly ground
black pepper or hot sauce,
as desired
½ teaspoon sugar (optional)

Preheat the broiler.

Cut off stem ends of garlic but leave the peel on. (This will make for easier peeling after broiling.)

Place the garlic cloves and the whole tomatoes in a shallow roasting pan. Broil 3 to 4 inches from heat for 7 minutes. Turn the tomatoes and garlic, and continue broiling until charred, about 6 minutes more. Remove from the heat and let the tomatoes sit in the pan; reserve juices.

Transfer the garlic cloves to a chopping board; let sit until cool enough to handle, about 1 minute.

Peel and mash or mince the garlic cloves by hand or in a food processor; transfer to a large bowl.

Working over the bowl to catch juices, peel the tomatoes. (The peel will be blackened and split, and will be easy to slip off.) Discard peels.

Core the tomatoes. Finely chop tomatoes by hand or in a food processor. Transfer to bowl with garlic; add any juices from the broiler pan. Stir in the oil, salt, pepper, and sugar, if desired. Serve over hot pasta.

Makes about 4 cups,
or eight ½-cup servings

Helpful Hint

Depending on the ripeness and juiciness of the tomatoes, the sauce may be thin. The sauce may be thickened by boiling it gently until it reaches the desired consistency, or by adding a ½ cup of freshly grated Parmesan or Romano cheese when tossing with the hot cooked pasta. (Adding cheese will increase the fat content, however.)

Per Serving:
47 Calories; 1g Protein; 4g Fat;
4g Carbohydrates; 0 Cholesterol;
151mg Sodium; 1g Fiber.

Pesto-Style Sauce

*Serve this delicious sauce over your favorite pasta
or prepare Capellini, Pepper, and Pesto Toss (page 49).*

2 tablespoons olive oil
4 cloves garlic, minced
1½ tablespoons all-purpose
    flour
One 14½-ounce can vegetable
    broth
2 cups packed, fresh basil
    leaves
¼ teaspoon salt, or to taste
¼ teaspoon freshly ground
    black pepper
¼ cup freshly grated Parmesan
    cheese

Heat the oil in a medium saucepan over medium heat. Add garlic, and cook, stirring, 2 minutes. Sprinkle with flour, and cook, stirring, 1 minute. Slowly stir in vegetable broth; bring to a simmer, stirring occasionally.

Finely chop the basil by hand or in a food processor. Add the basil, salt, and pepper to the sauce, reduce the heat to low, and simmer 2 minutes. Remove from heat and stir in cheese. Serve over hot pasta. Refrigerate up to 3 days or freeze up to 3 months.

**Makes about 2 cups,
or four ½-cup servings**

Per Serving:
112 Calories; 4g Protein; 9g Fat;
6g Carbohydrates; 4mg Cholesterol;
693mg Sodium; 0 Fiber.

Provençal Rouille for Pasta

This rouille, adapted from the French pantheon of velvety sauces,
is best served over a filled-pasta dish such as ravioli, tortellini,
or manicotti. Made with leftover bread, rouille is a culinary
ode to sweet red peppers (and ingenuity).

**4 thick slices of French or
   Italian bread, crusts
   removed**
**1½ cups diced roasted sweet
   peppers (one 12-ounce jar)**
**2 tablespoons olive oil or
   canola oil**
2 cloves garlic, minced
½ teaspoon dried thyme
¼ teaspoon cayenne pepper
¼ teaspoon salt
½ cup low-fat milk or soy milk
¼ cup chopped fresh parsley

In a medium mixing bowl, soak
the bread in warm water for about
5 seconds. Place the bread in a
colander, drain, and gently
squeeze out the excess water like a
sponge.

Transfer the mass of bread to a
blender or food processor fitted
with a steel blade. Add the sweet
peppers, oil, garlic, thyme,
cayenne, and salt. Process the
mixture until smooth, about
5 seconds. Transfer the sauce to a
medium saucepan and stir in the
milk. Bring the sauce to a simmer
over medium heat, stirring
occasionally.

When ready, ladle the rouille
over cooked pasta and garnish
with parsley.

**Makes 3 cups,
or six ½-cup servings**

Per Serving:
106 Calories; 3g Protein; 5g Fat;
12g Carbohydrates; 1mg Cholesterol;
211mg Sodium; 1g Fiber.

Roasted Pepper Diablo Sauce

This piquant diablo sauce is the marriage of Italian marinara with the roasted chili peppers favored in Mexican and Southwestern cuisine. (Diablo, or diavolo, loosely means "devil" in Italian.)

2 to 3 large poblano or New
   Mexico chili peppers
1 tablespoon olive oil
1 medium yellow onion, diced
2 cloves garlic, minced
One 28-ounce can plum
   tomatoes
¼ cup chopped fresh parsley
1 teaspoon dried oregano
1 teaspoon dried basil
½ teaspoon salt
¼ teaspoon red pepper flakes

Preheat the broiler.

Place the chilies on a baking pan. Place the pan beneath the broiler and broil until the skins are nearly charred and flaky, about 5 minutes. Turn the peppers and broil until the other side is charred, about 5 minutes more. Remove the peppers from the heat and let cool slightly. With a knife, scrape off any charred or flaky spots. Dice the flesh.

Meanwhile, in a large saucepan, heat the oil over medium heat. Add the onion and garlic and cook, stirring, for 4 minutes. Add the plum tomatoes, parsley, and seasonings and bring to a simmer. Reduce the heat to low and cook for 15 to 20 minutes, stirring occasionally. Add the roasted chilies to the sauce about 5 minutes before the sauce has finished cooking.

Transfer the sauce to a blender or food processor fitted with a steel blade and process until smooth, 5 to 10 seconds. Ladle the sauce over the cooked pasta.

Per Serving:
73 Calories; 2g Protein; 2g Fat;
9g Carbohydrates; 0 Cholesterol;
483mg Sodium; 3g Fiber.

**Makes 3 cups,
or six ½-cup servings**

Neapolitan Tomato Sauce

*This chunky vegetable-tomato sauce is so good you'll want
to eat it by the spoonful. It makes a rustic topping for
a soothing supper of spaghetti or linguine.*

1 tablespoon olive oil
2 medium carrots, chopped
**1 medium yellow or other
    sweet onion, diced**
1 stalk celery, diced
2 cloves garlic, minced
**One 28-ounce can plum toma-
    toes or stewed tomatoes**
2 tablespoons tomato paste
1 tablespoon dried parsley
2 teaspoons dried oregano
1 teaspoon dried basil
**½ teaspoon freshly ground
    black pepper**
½ teaspoon salt

In a large saucepan, heat the oil
over medium heat. Add the
carrots, onion, celery, and garlic
and cook, stirring, until the
vegetables are tender, 6 to
7 minutes.

Add all of the remaining
ingredients, and bring to a
simmer. Cook for about 15 minutes
over medium-low heat, stirring
occasionally. As the sauce cooks,
use the edge of a spoon to break
up the chunks of tomatoes.

When ready to eat, ladle the
sauce over plates of cooked pasta.

**Makes 2 cups,
or four ½-cup servings**

Per Serving:
68 Calories; 2g Protein; 2g Fat;
10g Carbohydrates; 0 Cholesterol;
424mg Sodium; 2g Fiber.

181

Chunky Mushroom and Garlic Tomato Sauce

Using medium-high heat and a heavy saucepan will quickly caramelize the onion and seal in the mushrooms' natural juices. Crushing the fennel seeds between your fingers just before adding them to the sauce will bring out the fragrant anise flavor.

2 tablespoons olive oil
1 large yellow or other sweet
   onion, coarsely chopped
8 ounces cremini or button
   mushrooms, quartered
4 cloves garlic, minced
One 28-ounce can crushed
   tomatoes
¼ cup dry red wine or water
¾ teaspoon fennel seeds,
   slightly crushed
¼ teaspoon red pepper flakes
¼ teaspoon sugar (optional)

Heat the oil in a large, heavy saucepan over medium-high heat. Add the onion and cook, stirring, 5 minutes. Add the mushrooms and garlic and cook, stirring, 3 minutes more. Add the tomatoes, wine or water, fennel seeds, pepper flakes, and, if desired, sugar. Bring to a boil, then immediately reduce heat until simmering. Simmer, uncovered, stirring frequently, until slightly thickened, 10 to 12 minutes. Serve over hot pasta.

Sauce will keep in the refrigerator up to 5 days or for up to 3 months in the freezer.

**Makes 5 cups,
or ten ½-cup servings**

Per Serving:
45 Calories; 1g Protein; 3g Fat;
4g Carbohydrates; 0 Cholesterol;
22mg Sodium; 1g Fiber.

Fresh No-Cook Tomato-Ricotta Sauce

*This recipe demands flavorful fresh tomatoes. If regular tomatoes
are not in season, substitute ripe plum tomatoes.*

**1 pound very ripe red or yellow
tomatoes (2 large or
3 medium tomatoes)**
1 cup part-skim ricotta cheese
**⅓ cup chopped fresh basil,
chives, or mixed fresh herbs**
**2 tablespoons garlic-infused
olive oil**
**2 tablespoons balsamic vinegar
or white balsamic vinegar**
½ teaspoon salt, or to taste
**¼ teaspoon freshly ground
black pepper**

Place a strainer over a large bowl.
Cut the tomatoes in half crosswise,
and squeeze the juice and seeds
into the strainer. With a wooden
spoon, press on the seeds to
extract all of the juice; discard
seeds.

Add the ricotta, herbs, oil,
vinegar, salt, and pepper to the
tomato juice. Coarsely chop the
tomatoes and add them to the
bowl. Toss well.

Toss the sauce with hot cooked
pasta of your choice. Sauce may
be covered and chilled up to 8
hours before serving. Let stand at
room temperature 30 minutes
before tossing with hot pasta.
Serve with additional black
pepper, if desired.

**Makes 2½ cups,
or five ½-cup servings**

Per Serving:
127 Calories; 8g Protein; 7g Fat;
8g Carbohydrates; 8mg Cholesterol;
320mg Sodium; 1g Fiber.

Veracruz Sauce

This tangy sauce will remind you of the best in Mexican cuisine. For a spicier sauce, stir in a minced chipotle chili or two. Look for canned chipotle chilies in adobo sauce at Mexican grocery stores or in the ethnic section of some supermarkets.

2 tablespoons vegetable or olive oil
1 medium sweet or red onion, chopped
4 cloves garlic, minced
One 14½-ounce can Mexican or salsa-style stewed tomatoes, undrained
One 10½-ounce can tomatoes with green chilies, undrained
¼ cup pitted chopped green Spanish or pimiento-stuffed olives
1 tablespoon drained capers
½ cup coarsely chopped cilantro

Heat the oil in a large saucepan over medium heat. Add the onion and cook, stirring, 5 minutes. Add the garlic and cook, stirring, 2 minutes more. Add the stewed tomatoes, tomatoes with green chilies, olives, and capers.

Bring to a boil, then immediately reduce the heat to a simmer. Simmer, uncovered, stirring occasionally, until slightly thickened, about 10 minutes.

Remove from heat; stir in cilantro. Serve over hot pasta.

Sauce may be prepared up to 3 days in advance.

Makes 3½ cups, or seven ½-cup servings

Per Serving:
87 Calories; 1g Protein; 5g Fat; 8g Carbohydrates; 0 Cholesterol; 489mg Sodium; 1g Fiber.

Mole-Style Tomato Sauce

*Unsweetened chocolate, chili powder, cinnamon, and toasted almonds give
this quick-cooking mole sauce an authentic Mexican flavor.*

¼ cup sliced almonds
1 tablespoon vegetable oil
1 medium onion, chopped
3 cloves garlic, minced
One 15-ounce can tomato sauce
¼ cup water
1 tablespoon chili powder
1 teaspoon unsweetened cocoa
½ teaspoon cinnamon
¼ teaspoon sugar

Heat a large, deep skillet over
medium heat until hot. Add the
almonds and cook, shaking the
skillet frequently, until almonds
are lightly toasted and fragrant,
2 to 3 minutes. Pour onto a
chopping board to cool.

Add the oil and onion to the
same skillet and cook, stirring,
until the onion is tender, about
6 minutes. Add the garlic and
cook, stirring, 1 minute more.

Add all of the remaining
ingredients; bring to a simmer,
stirring occasionally. Finely chop
the toasted almonds and add them
to the sauce. Serve over hot pasta.

The sauce may be stored in the
refrigerator for up to 3 days or in
the freezer for 3 months.

**Makes 2 cups,
or four ½-cup servings**

Per Serving:
135 Calories; 4g Protein; 8g Fat;
14g Carbohydrates; 0 Cholesterol;
652mg Sodium; 4g Fiber.

Spicy Asian Sauce

Serve this tasty sauce over hot cooked Chinese curly noodles or vermicelli. If desired, add mixed Asian vegetables to the pasta cooking water during the last several minutes of pasta cooking time. Look for black bean garlic sauce or paste in the Chinese food section of your supermarket.

Two 14½-ounce cans vegetable broth
2 tablespoons black bean garlic sauce or paste
¼ teaspoon ground white pepper or ½ teaspoon freshly ground black pepper
¾ cup water
¼ cup cornstarch
½ cup chopped cilantro
1 tablespoon dark or "toasted" sesame oil

Combine the broth, garlic sauce, and pepper in a medium saucepan. Bring to a boil over high heat, then immediately reduce the heat to low. Simmer, uncovered, for 5 minutes.

In a small bowl, combine the water and cornstarch until smooth. Stir it into the broth mixture and return to a simmer. Simmer until sauce thickens, stirring occasionally, about 2 minutes.

Remove from the heat; stir in the cilantro and sesame oil. Serve over hot pasta.

The sauce can be prepared up to 3 days in advance.

Makes 4 cups, or eight ½-cup servings

Per Serving:
48 Calories; 2g Protein; 2g Fat;
5g Carbohydrates; 0 Cholesterol;
431mg Sodium; 0 Fiber.

Index

187

Photo by Emily Solomon

Photo by Stuart Rodgers Ltd.

For more than a decade **Jay Solomon** has been cooking with flair and entertaining with gusto. A cookbook author and chef, Solomon has written twelve cookbooks and is the author of *Vegetarian Times Vegetarian Entertaining*. His recipes and articles have appeared in magazines and newspapers across the country, including *Vegetarian Times* magazine. A graduate of Cornell University's School of Hotel Administration, Solomon is the owner of Jay's Cafe, a popular restaurant in Ithaca, New York.

Karen A. Levin, a cookbook author and food consultant, has specialized in recipe development for the past seventeen years. She has written numerous cookbooks for major food companies and is the author of *Twenty Minute Chicken Dishes, Meatless Dishes in Twenty Minutes, The Twenty Minute Low Fat Gourmet,* and *The Twenty Minute One Dish Gourmet* (Contemporary Books). Ms. Levin is a contributor to *Cooking Light, Vegetarian Times,* and *Health* magazines.

to learn more about
low-fat and healthy living
month after month...

SUBSCRIBE TO

❑ **8 issues $19.95** ❑ **12 issues (1 year) $29.95**

C7LFBT

SAVE 29% OFF THE COVER PRICE

NAME   (PLEASE PRINT)

ADDRESS   APT.

CITY/STATE/ZIP

❑ Payment enclosed   ❑ Please bill me   Offer good in US only

---

▲ **FOR YOU**   ▼ **FOR A FRIEND**

---

to learn more about
low-fat and healthy living
month after month...

SUBSCRIBE TO

❑ **8 issues $19.95** ❑ **12 issues (1 year) $29.95**

C7LFBB

SAVE 29% OFF THE COVER PRICE

NAME   (PLEASE PRINT)

ADDRESS   APT.

CITY/STATE/ZIP

❑ Payment enclosed   ❑ Please bill me   Offer good in US only

BUSINESS REPLY MAIL

FIRST-CLASS MAIL   PERMIT NO. 106   FLAGLER BEACH FL

POSTAGE WILL BE PAID BY ADDRESSEE

Vegetarian
T I M E S

PO BOX 420166
PALM COAST FL 32142-9107

BUSINESS REPLY MAIL

FIRST-CLASS MAIL   PERMIT NO. 106   FLAGLER BEACH FL

POSTAGE WILL BE PAID BY ADDRESSEE

Vegetarian
T I M E S

PO BOX 420166
PALM COAST FL 32142-9107